Survival Alliances

Survival Alliances

BECAUSE THERE'S SAFETY IN NUMBERS

Beth Stone

ISBN-13: 9780692925324
ISBN-10: 0692925325

Acknowledgement

'd like to dedicate this book to my children, my daughters-in-law and my grandchildren who have been the source of motivation for most of my preparedness efforts.

Special thanks to my husband, Alan, for all he has done as we have worked together to share our knowledge with others.

I would also like to acknowledge Michelle Stott who designed our logo and Kenny Mock, of Mended Hearts Music, who designed our book cover. Special thanks to Curtis Markham for his editing assistance. All have been a great help and source of support. Alan and I are grateful for their encouragement.

I also wish to express my gratitude to the many people who have allowed us to share their journey to preparedness. Their desire to prepare their families has affirmed our enthusiasm for this work.

Table of Contents

Foreword

At 6:45 am the house lights flickered and then went out. The morning is cool for June and the air outside is filled with the sounds of people in my neighborhood leaving for work and traffic from a nearby main street. I am awaiting my daughter's arrival. I dog-sit while she is in class. As I wait, I knock off some morning chores, but it is dark enough in some parts of the house that I need a lantern. Not wanting to do chores by lantern light that could wait until sunup; I stick to the rooms with more windows and wait. As time passes I begin wondering why the power is out. There has been no bad weather or high winds that usually accompany such outages. As I wait, my thoughts wander to a slightly different scenario:

At 6:45 am the house lights flicker and then go out. The morning is cool for June and it is eerily quiet for this time of the morning. Usually the sounds of people leaving their homes for work and traffic from a nearby main street fill the air. Now the sound of morning birds is all I hear. I pick up the phone to call the electric company to report the outage. I always worry that no one will for a while, thinking someone else has already done it. There is no dial tone. I try my cell phone. It's dead despite having charged all night. I begin walking through the house and realize the smoke detectors aren't making that annoying chirping sound. Even the hall night lights which have battery backup are out.

At 8am a good friend and neighbor, Carla, knocks on my door. She couldn't reach me by phone, so she decided to drive over. She turns the key, but nothing happens. Frustrated, she smacks her fist on the steering wheel. As she sat there thinking of what do, her next-door neighbor pecked on her car window. The neighbor tells Carla that her car won't start either. As they stand in the driveway they notice that the street is filling with would be morning commuters. It is becoming obvious that is no ordinary black out. I invite her in and she asks the question that has been on my mind for the past hour," Do you think this is it? Has there been an EMP?"

For those who may not know what this is, an EMP (short for electro-magnetic pulse) is the result of a large solar flare or manmade weapon detonation. Either can destroy all electric circuitry not specially protected. Scientists, military and security experts have been warning of the dangers of EMPs and the effect they could have on our world. Currently, there are several antagonistic countries capable of detonating missiles carrying this technology miles above us. This would reduce us to an existence faced by Western pioneers in the United States. Experts in emergency planning estimate it could take at least a year to recover from such an attack or solar discharge. It's much longer if we don't have tremendous help from the global community and our nations' capital is affected. If we are affected coast to coast by a strong enemy or an alliance of aggressors – well, Heaven help us.

Snapping back to reality from my daydreaming, I begin to look around my home and take stock of things. I note the pile of sorted, but dirty laundry on the laundry room floor and the dishwasher I didn't start last night. I feel a rumble in my stomach and realize I will be eating a peanut butter sandwich and room temperature water for breakfast because I don't want to open my refrigerator if I don't have too. Depending on how long the power is out, I will appreciate a cold drink later, more than now. I am thankful I have food storage for my family and animals and ways to cook without electricity. Before my mind has time to wander further, the power comes on bringing the welcome feeling of my central air and ceiling fans.

How would you and your home fair during a blackout of a several days? What about the more common several hours due to bad weather or accident damaging power lines? Depending on where you live, there may be seasonal dangers such as hurricanes, tornados, or blizzards. Some areas are prone to earthquakes or wild fires. Have you considered the possibility of needing to shelter in place or even evacuate because of rioting and looting? What about long term unemployment, injury or illness. If you don't like the answer – read on.

Warning

Please read the entire book before discussing these concepts with anyone. Security topics are covered throughout and will help you decide what information you may wish to share and with whom.

Disclaimer

The information in this book is not a substitute for the services of an attorney, accountant, physician, or any other specialist. The reader assumes responsibility for their decisions and actions as they work toward emergency preparedness. There are medical and legal variables that are unique to the reader which may be contrary to the information contained in this book. Do your homework.

"Two are better than one... for if they fall, the one will lift up his fellow; But woe unto him that is alone when he falleth; for he hath not another to help him up."
—ECCLESIASTES 4:9-10

CHAPTER 1

The Evolution of a Concept

A Survival Alliance is a group of people who enter a cooperative relationship to maximize their chances of survival and success during emergencies, disasters, or times of danger. The power and safety of a prepared group greatly increases the chance that group members can weather any trial. This is the short answer to the questions, "What is a Survival Alliance and why do I need one?" The rest of this book is dedicated to the long answer.

While preparing to write this book, I realized that it was a series of learning experiences that led us to this point and changed how we looked at preparedness. One such experience was Hurricane Katrina. Although we lived in Oklahoma, we had good friends who lived in Louisiana. We met our friends at church and our sons were in the same Boy Scout Troop and high school. Her husband worked with my husband and they moved here shortly before we did. All their extended family lived in Louisiana and were dramatically affected by this terrible storm. After the storm passed, the men brought the children and their adult sister, who was visiting from college in Utah, to Oklahoma. They only stayed long enough to drop off the family and gather needed supplies and return home. They left one of the women behind to care for elderly grandparents who could not travel. She only had a few days of clean water and had sustained heavy damage to their property. She stayed because she was the only one with the necessary nursing skills to care for her grandparents. They told stories of suffocating, sweltering heat and humidity, of the total darkness, and lack of clean water. The fear of criminal activity and keeping their children safe was heart breaking to hear.

After saying goodbye to family, they loaded U-hauls with much needed donations from the good people of our town and headed back with help. My husband joined the other men who drove armed to protect their precious supplies from thugs. A book could be written on the lessons learned from Hurricane Katrina. It suffices to say that the news only covered a small portion of the problems and suffering that occurred there, and continues to this day.

When they returned, they told stories of taking turns guarding the property from thieves and looters, sleeping to the buzz of generators in the area and destruction like they had never seen before. The mud, filth, and smell of rotten food, vegetation, and animals were overwhelming. They saw many who had very humble homes and meager belongings left with nothing and without prospects. They also shared how, because of criminal activity in neighboring New Orleans, state and federal help was greatly delayed in helping Covington. Our friends' daughter, who is a remarkable young woman and a prepper, used food storage donated by members of our congregation and from her family's supply, to set up a kitchen in the driveway of the local fire station. She cooked nourishing dishes like red beans and rice for hungry neighbors for days. Her efforts, with the help from churches outside the state, were providing help long before the Red Cross and FEMA arrived.

As news of looting, depravity, and suffering was reported, my husband and I realized that we were not adequately prepared for how times of crisis can bring out the worst in people. We began rethinking our plans and our preparedness supplies.

Gaining Skills to Share

While serving as Welfare Service Missionaries for The Church of Jesus Christ of Latter Day Saints, we were assigned to our local Home Storage Center. Our experience as Emergency Preparedness Specialists in different congregations, where we had lived before, made this the perfect job for us. While serving there, we met many hardworking people who sincerely wanted to be prepared for emergencies and provide for the families. It was our pleasure to assist them in their efforts. One day the facility manager brought me a book that radically changed our preparedness viewpoint. **One Second After**, by William R. Forstchen, is an incredible example of prepper fiction at its' finest. The book opens with the detonation of several EMPs which destroys all electronic equipment not specially hardened and protected. In an instant America is plunged into the early 1800s. Through gripping story lines, ideas were brought to our attention that we had never thought of before. We began to contemplate what life would be like without technology and electricity for a prolonged time. (Also, look for the sequel books, **One Year After** and **The Final Day**. Awesome reads.) We considered how a situation like that would cause people to behave and what we needed to do to better prepare our family for the unexpected.

Next, the books **The Right to Bear Arms** by Mike Foster & **Patriots** by James Wesley Rawles, editor of www.SurvivalBlog.com, would further illustrate these concepts. I had been focused on emergency preparedness for many years and felt confident that we had things fairly well covered. I had never considered my inability to handle our needs due to **logistical constraints**. We simply did not have enough people in our family to do all that would be required in the most dangerous or prolonged emergencies. I had never given the tactical aspect of this arrangement much thought. Once I considered it in detail, I could see the profound wisdom of coming together as a group. We made plans to have our adult children, living in our area, join us with their families if we ever had a serious emergency.

As we were reading these books, I read an article about a soldier who served in the United States military in a former Soviet country. I can't remember his name or where he served, but recall that was during a recent civil war. I wish I could thank him for his service and the thought provoking interview he gave which inspired this book. In the interview, he was asked how people from the civilian population faired. He explained that large extended families living under one roof faired the best. He said that smaller families and individuals were quickly overrun by gangs looking for food and other provisions. They simply could not perform all the duties needed to maintain the household and provide security at the same time. The most successful groups were with their friends and loved ones and pooled resources to ensure everyone was ok. We reflected on how we could best use this information and got to work.

Our family bought five acres a little outside of town. We put a great deal of effort into developing the property to sustain our family. We aren't hippies or come from farming families, but being prepared for the unexpected was important to us. We also had developed an appreciation for what nature and preparedness skills could do for our growing boys and grand kids. We planted a variety of fruit trees and grapes, created raised garden beds, and raised chickens, goats, and donkeys. We had a water well and water storage, and extensive food supplies. We had accumulated all the tools necessary for communal gardening, stock piled seeds, and gathered materials for fencing to protecting our crops. We acquired hand tools for construction and had a significant amount of lumber and firewood. We had firearms and ammunition for hunting and self-defense. We estimated that we had a year supply of food and other necessities for the nine people in our family group.

Our family has always been geared toward preparedness. Living these principles has been a blessing of peace and reassurance for us throughout almost thirty years of marriage. We have used our reserves to weather unexpected expenses, blizzards, tornados, and have shared with family and strangers in need.

In addition to our preparedness measures, we read and watch a lot of news. Monitoring global political and economic news and how weather trends are affecting the worlds' food supply lets us adjust our preparedness accordingly. Most of the news and information we base these decisions on are outside mainstream outlets. The internet makes it very easy to research almost anything in great detail. There is an abundance of great websites, blogs, and pod casts often that break news and sound alarms long before the mainstream media. This information can help you stay ahead of price increases and shortages of items you store.

I was familiar with the lone wolf concept which describes the belief that a single person can move about and function more efficiently than a group. I was also knowledgeable about the notion of taking my immediate family to a predetermined and prepared location. This is commonly referred to as **bugging out**. The last option I knew of was **sheltering in place**. Prior to reading this interview, this was the option that seemed best for our family. After taking this interview into consideration, we developed multiple options and plans within a community of likeminded people.

CHAPTER 2

The Case for Emergency Preparedness

After reading several books, we began to create a systematic response plan for our family and select friends. It was drastically different than our previous plans and before we knew it, the **Survival Alliance Method** was born. After a year, we knew we needed to share this concept with as many people as would listen, but where to start? Writing a book seemed the obvious answer. As I developed the chapters, I included what we learned as we created our own survival alliance. We met others who were preparing to "circle the wagons" with family and friends with whom we swapped ideas and helped address difficult issues. Their wisdom was included as well.

The beginning is always the best place to start anything, but we realize many of our readers already understand the need to be prepared. What they may lack is an efficient way to organize themselves. For this reason, what follows is an abbreviated discussion of basic preparedness. The internet is a great source for further information on basic preparedness. If nothing else, maybe some of what follows will be helpful in persuading a friend or family member to lean toward your way of thinking.

We live in a world of uncertainty. As the old saying goes, "The only thing that is constant is change." Despite this, when most people think of preppers, they envision end of world destruction or a zombie apocalypse. Hollywood has done a great disservice to the image of those who prepare for bumps in the road of life. People who set aside food, extra toilet paper, medicine, or ammunition are often portrayed as crazies. While there are some preppers who may be obsessive about their efforts, the same can be said about the way some people approach their jobs or hobbies. Unfortunately, a few rotten apples spoil the basket for everyone. Most so called preppers are average, hardworking, people of faith, who just want to take care of themselves and their families. A generation or two ago this was considered a responsible, adult approach to life.

We often say that we are preparing for the unexpected, but how many of the things we prepare for are truly unexpected? Is there really anyone that thinks they can't be injured, lose their job, experience a prolonged illness, or lose a loved one? Does anyone believe their tires won't go flat, vehicles don't breakdown, or that houses repair themselves? Many people have auto insurance, health insurance, life insurance, savings accounts, and even burial policies. It is considered the responsible thing to do. Those same people eat, use household products, and take over the counter medications on occasion; and yet, they do not think that these everyday necessities could be interrupted. Even nature brings events like thunderstorms, tornados, snow storms, or hurricanes which can lead to power outages. Any of these circumstances can have an impact on an individual or their family. Disasters can be life changing and lead to physical, financial, and emotional hardship. Despite this, there seems to be a disconnect between these two belief structures. On one hand, many prepare for certain events and consider these efforts normal. On the other hand, the same people completely often ignore the need to prepare for other things they know can happen. What causes this disconnect? I believe we will prepare for those things we are told to prepare for. This is especially true of things for which there is a legal or monetary penalty for failure to do so. We are less likely to prepare for things that are not regulated, even when they make sense. That seems foolish and yet those that are prepared are the ones ridiculed.

In the event of a natural disaster, civil unrest, economic collapse, an EMP, or other such disruption in your life, your top priority will be the well-being of those you love. I can't imagine being separated from my family and friends and wondering if they are safe. I would be worried and distracted while trying to deal with my own circumstances. I also can't imagine how my husband and

I would "hold down the fort" alone. The simple and practical answer is to plan to be together for a major emergency and **form a Survival Alliance**.

The concept is based on the idea that there is safety in numbers, but numbers alone aren't all that matters. A successful Survival Alliance requires a balance of numbers, skills, personalities, preps, and planning. I will take each one of these points and share what we have learned, how it works for us, and give you options to choose from. This will allow you to customize your survival alliance to your needs and values. The ideas I share are certainly not the only ways to do things. My hope is to provide food for thought and inspire you to create an alliance tailored to your needs.

As we have seen in recent years, the world has become a more dangerous place. Terrorism, racial tension, police shootings, and rising crime rates make it necessary for citizens to take more responsibility for their own safety and well-being. Events such as recession, ice storms, earthquakes and drought affect us in ways that make it necessary to be able to feed ourselves from our own stores. Being prepared to care for yourself, family and home in situations of varying durations is a prudent choice.

One of the most important things you can do, when trying to become more prepared, is anticipate emergencies and plan accordingly. This concept is illustrated in the technique called Defensive Driving. Using this philosophy, drivers are encouraged to be alert to what is happening around them as they drive and anticipate hazards. If you find yourself behind a truck pulling a load of pipe, consider what you would do if his load spilled. This might result in you changing lanes or simply putting some space between you. If you notice a car beside you weaving a bit in their lane, you can slow or pass them in case they are intoxicated or distracted by the phone or other passengers. If you notice a popular intersection ahead, you can slow a bit and be alert for drivers who forget to signal before turning. This is a proactive approach to driving and saves countless people from accidents and death every year. This technique involves situational awareness and hazard mitigation which can be applied to preparedness. We created categories for emergencies and suggested actions.

Level I – Common Short Term Emergencies

These are events that are part of everyday and seasonal life. These types of problems include storm related power outage, water supply disruption due to water main breaks or water quality alerts, seasonal weather events such as thunderstorm, tornado, hurricane, winter events, an evacuation due to fire, train derailment, or criminal activity in the area. These events range from hours up to a week.

Level II – Intermediate Duration Events

These are events that, while not seasonal or cyclical, are not outside the realm of reasonable possibility. If you follow current events, political and economic trends can often anticipate these types of events. There could be disruption of transportation of goods due to labor strike, global or domestic economic crisis such as a stock market crash and resulting hyperinflation, epidemic or pandemic disease, terrorism, or political events. At this level, investments may suffer significant losses as connected markets react poorly to the crisis. Paper money could become devalued. What follows would be a cascading effect on our economy which could lead to panic, civil unrest, and rioting. These events can also have lingering effects for several months *if* they do not continue to escalate.

Level III - Protracted Length Events

These are many of the same events as Level II, but instead of being resolved in a relatively short time, the disrupting factors increase and spread for several months. Domestic terrorism in multiple coordinated strikes will cause destabilizing social, economic, and infrastructure damage that continue in duration. Continued duration would lead to panic, civil disobedience and violent protests as well as a significant increase in theft and violent crime. Tangible assets in the form of precious metals, foods, sundry items, and ammunition are stripped from shelves to unload nearly worthless currency for personal consumption and barter. Credit would be a convenience of the past.

Level IV - Long Term Civil Disruption with realistic hope of recovery

This refers to a break down in some normal city, state and/or federal services that are temporarily disrupted. Lasting up to three months, there is some central power or regional organization and aid. There is realistic hope for normalization, despite initial chaos. Services affected might include trash pick-up, water treatment and sewage maintenance, electric and gas, communication, law enforcement, medical services, banking, shopping, transportation, and fuel supply. At this point, you may want to live in communal groups for protection and to pool resources. An EMP strike or solar flare, catastrophic economic collapse, declaration of war by a foreign power, and natural disasters are all possible causes. City, state, and even federal resources and institutions will be over-whelmed and will struggle to function. Depending on the time of year and duration, disruption of public utilities and sanitation services would lead to an untold number of deaths in the civilian population. A combination of Level II and III events can cascade into long term civil disruption or continue to Level IV.

Level V – Long term Civil Disruption with no foreseen formal recovery

This is the least likely scenario, but it's better to have contemplated it and never use your plans than need to act and be unprepared. This level presumes rule of law and centralized power has been indefinitely disrupted. Citizens are on their own. This may be due to foreign invasion or an EMP which would affect the entire nation. Gangs will grow into organized mobs that prey on anyone who can't repel them. Disease, starvation, and exposure will kill large portions of the population. Early recognition of this type of event and swift action is critical.

Knowing what to do in the event of an emergency is half the battle. Being prepared before it happens is the other. Making the best use of resources and purchasing critical supplies as quickly as possible can mean the difference between life and death, security and danger. Here are some suggestions for preparing and responding to each level of emergency. Consider how you would deal with any of these scenarios. A Survival Alliance makes these situations easier and safer.

Level I and 2 Preparation Ideas

- 72-hour kit / bug out bag
- Weather radio
- First Aid Kit
- Hygiene: 2 months of toilet paper, wipes, Kleenex, body/ foot powder, feminine hygiene items
- Hand crank powered radio, rechargeable power bricks for personal devices,
- Portable cook stove and fuel such as Sterno or propane, barbeque grill, fire starters, matches, charcoal, and firewood
- 3 gallons per person per day X 7 days (1- drinking, 2 – washing/cooking) Consider a combination of 5 and 1 gallon jugs, and individual bottled water. Add 55-gallon water barrels for families.
- Portable water filter such as Seychelle or Life Straw
- Tissues, toilet paper, baby wipes, paper napkins and disposable plates, cups, etc.

Extra prescription & OTC medicines, sunscreen, insect repellant & first aid supplies

Level 3 Preparation Ideas

- Items from Level I and 2 list
- Three months of short term food and 3 months long term food
- Three months drinking water – plus extra for hygiene & cooking
- Additional fuel for warmth and cooking

- Pandemic supplies for 3 months
- Self-defense equipment and weapons, firearms, ammunition, extra magazines and bandoliers, scopes, cleaning kits and spare parts.
- Seasonal clothing: Layered warmth for winter with extra gloves and head wear and high performance, moisture wicking fabrics for tops and bottom & wool blend sock, shorts with cargo pockets or zip-off pants, hats with sun brim and sunglasses
- Ham radio and accessories with solar recharger and batteries
- Filter masks – general particle and viral protection types, medical and work gloves
- Family tent and 2-man tent for gear. Sleeping outside is often cooler.
- Gasoline (if it can be stored safely) – recommend 40 gallons and stabilizer
- Clothes line and pins, low suds laundry detergent or bars, rub board and tub or 5-gallon bucket or manual bucket agitator set up, clothes wringer
- Long term food storage
- Electric and solar powered battery charger with appropriate batteries
- Seeds and containers for planting, basic tools and gardening guide
- Garden tools, diatomaceous earth,
- Knives for butchering and skinning
- Medical glue, Steri-strips, and suture kits / staplers
- Childbirth kit and newborn supplies if of childbearing age
- Manual grain mill and meat grinder and accessories, canning supplies
- Firewood and Duraflame* logs for fireplace, chimaera, barbecue grill or rocket stove, ax and machete. *Duraflame should only be used for warmth, not for cooking over.
- Various light sources for different tasks: flash light, cylume light sticks, lantern, candles
- Solar / electric power banks and cords for recharging phones and tablets
- Provisions for dealing with all forms of waste – trash bags of various sizes, 5 gallon buckets, metal burn barrel, agricultural lime and shovels for digging holes
- Establish routine health care and prepare trauma response
- Observe highest level security and defensive measures

At the first indication that an event is likely to result in service disruption, purchase items that you are still lacking. Obvious supplies such as flashlights, hand warmers, candles and batteries may be in short supply very quickly, so try to keep those items stocked up. There will be long lines as most people only have a day or two worth of food in their homes. There could be squabbles over items such as bottled water, first aid kits, soda, milk, eggs, and bread. If you need or want more, but the supplies are low or you want to avoid grocery stores, consider purchasing alternative forms of the items or their ingredients. Few would think to buy paraffin (in the canning section of most grocery stores), wicks from camping or craft stores, glow sticks from the party stores or section, food prep gloves found in restaurant/ party supply section or stores. Food service gloves can be used for handling dirty items, serving food, reducing the need to wash your hands during food prep (saves water) and toileting cleanup. Do not use these in place of medical gloves. Bleach or peroxide makes excellent disinfectants and manual can openers aren't even on the radar for the average Joe. Buying these types of items can position you with a surplus of supplies and allow you to share and/or barter with others.

Depending upon the type and level of emergency you are experiencing, you may be free of any concern for your safety or need to be vigilant and prepared to defend yourself while acquiring additional food or supplies. In some instances, no one may be concerned yet about the event you are preparing for, leaving you to shop undisturbed. In other situations, you may find store parking lots resemble a Black Friday sale and the store filled with nervous and rude customers. Still other situations may include looters, muggings, and car jackings. You will need to adjust your decision making and tactics to reflect real time events. If you do go out to purchase items or travel to help friends, keep your concerns to yourself when they could create panic. There is a line from the movie Men in Black that illustrates this point. "A person is smart. People are dumb." If you had the luxury of a one on one conversation with someone you knew or felt moved to share information with, it would probably be a safe decision that would be a blessing to them. However, well intentioned warnings to anxious strangers in public places can create hysteria. People are often emboldened in groups to do things they would normally not do alone. This mob mentality has resulted in shocking acts of criminal behavior after natural disasters, perceived social injustice, and political disagreement.

Some may think it's unfair for those with knowledge of what is happening to not let others know. While I can see the point, it's a matter of maintaining order and personal safety. People who are already in a store making purchases likely have a limited budget for preps. Many are not willing or able to make the type of purchase they should. If frightened, recent events have shown that robbery and looting frequently occur. This behavior deprives law abiding citizens of the resource sooner than had if people had remained relatively unaware and calm. By the time the average citizen figures out what's going on it will be too late, but those who have been vigilant and made sacrifices to be prepared are set. Eventually, everyone will figure it out. From that point on, avoid stores if possible. Despite this, if you wait too long into the crisis to prepare, it will be too dangerous.

As panic sets in, people will become desperate. Even good people can become frightened to the point of behaving irrationally. Criminals don't need an excuse. Many businesses will be closed due to power outage or vandalism, or because they lack personnel. One of the benefits of being prepared is having a well-stocked supply within your own home. If you cannot or do not wish to leave your home, you do not feel pressure to do so. Consider storing or purchasing some of the items on the list below. Many of these are items whose value is not generally understood. Generalized failure to understand the **long-term value** of items such as these, may make them much easier for you to find, even during panic buying.

- Fabric, sewing supplies, and patterns
- Sharpening stones, lubricating oil, scissor sharpener
- Entertainment items; games, books, puzzles, sporting goods
- Axes, hammers, saws, nails, screws,
- Electrical tape, needle nose pliers, zip ties
- Can openers, canning jars, lids, pectin, pickling spice and salt
- Paraffin from the craft or canning section,
- Rope, para-cord, carabiners, and clips from camping
- Shovels, plastic sheeting, contractor bags, staple guns /staples and duct tape
- 2x4s and other lumber, shingles, concrete mix, sand, and sand bags

As you can see, there are lots of possible scenarios to be prepared for. If not careful, it would be easy to become overwhelmed and let fear govern your thought process. It is important to keep your emotions in check. The Bible tells us, "God hath not given us the spirit of fear, but of power, and love and a sound mind." 2 Timothy 1:7. Set reasonable goals for yourself and be reasonable about the requirements you set for admission to your Survival Alliance. Every individual and family has different starting points and budgets. They will have unique talents and short comings, as you do. Regardless of what you ask of those joining your group, remember that you will need one another. Choose wisely. I know that if you are prayerful about your efforts, God will help you to know what is best for you and your family. The Spirit will prompt you and lead you as you make decisions. We have found this to be true in our lives as well as those of the many people we have met and worked with. We have been blessed with amazing finds of items we needed, sales, and even giveaways that have filled holes in our inventory. Many we have worked with have shared similar stories of promptings to look in a store or classified ads or stop at a garage sale to find exactly what they needed within their budget. I know that the Lord wants us to be successful in caring for our families. If we draw near to Him, He will draw near to us in our journey to preparedness.

CHAPTER 3
Getting Started at Home

Preparedness is a mindset and a way of life. It is the supreme assertion of personal independence and responsibility. I'm not talking about packing up the family and moving to the mountains or woods to live off the land. While there's something adventurous about that, most people just want to stay home. I'm talking about something more realistic for the average family. Of all the activities I've tried, none have had the value and long lasting satisfaction as those that foster self-reliance. Accepting responsibility for acquiring your basic needs and then doing something to secure those needs is very empowering and incredibly satisfying. A new pair of heels or decorative item for my home is nice; and if the shoes are from my favorite maker and on sale – very nice. The difference is that shoe shopping, for example, is not something that blesses my family. In fact, depending on your shopping habits, the new shoes may not even make *you* happy for long. It's a temporary thrill and distraction from the grind and rarely more. Now, don't get me wrong; I am not saying you shouldn't have nice things or enjoy vacations. It's a matter of balance. If you have not addressed the issues that could endanger your home, health, finances, or safety, whatever else you have done is misdirected effort. Securing the basic needs for yourself and family come first, and then, the rest can be enjoyed even more.

Many families have said that the activities they began to be more self-reliant, eliminate debt, or learn life skills turned out to be wonderful family or individual hobbies. Here are some examples:

- Gardening – container, plot, or acreage
- Walking, hiking and parkour
- Martial arts or self-defense training
- Raising chickens, rabbits, goats, hogs etc.
- Scouting and outdoor skill acquisition
- Cooking, grilling, canning and baking
- Carpentry projects, construction or repair skills
- Automotive and small engine repair

So, as you begin creating your own Survival Alliance, look for ways to learn new things. Have fun and spend more time with the people you love and enjoy being with. I know from our own experience and the testimonies of others, that there are many opportunities for wonderful memory making and fun along the way. Getting your ducks in a row can be challenging, but also very rewarding.

When given much thought, there are lots of reasons to motivate most people to begin preparing for the unexpected. Even if you don't have concerns about an impending economic collapse or an EMP, it just makes sense to hedge the effects of inflation on your ability to eat and feed your family. What about allergy medicine and tissues or toothpaste? Buying extra when there's a good sale and rotating stock so nothing goes to waste can become a habit, which requires little thought. The latest handbag, flashy rims for the truck, or frequent, expensive vacations are nice; but the satisfaction passes quickly. The credit card statement comes, bills are due and the mortgage needs to be paid. Living beyond your means and having little real substance to show for it comes at a heavy price. In many cases, a serious expense such a major automotive repair, serious illness or injury or unemployment pushes a budget to the breaking point. The stress and worry are the burdens that rob the joy from life. The peace of mind that comes from a low debt life style and a reserve stock of supplies is what can help you sleep at night. A trip to Disney or an island get away every few years is nice and creates wonderful memories, but if you lose your job or the power is out for 3 weeks after a natural disaster – you can't eat your pictures. Think of how much food, toilet paper, shampoo and diapers you could buy with half of the vacation money some spend yearly.

Food

Everyone needs to eat. An average person can go about three weeks without food. Heavier adults can go longer than those who are lighter or children can. How long depends on your activity level and your health at the time. Can you imagine not eating for three weeks? Even worse is watching your children go hungry. Food storage is **food insurance** against going without or spending money when the budget is tight.

Additionally, I'm sure you've noticed that food isn't getting cheaper. Generally, food costs more today than it did two years ago, and will cost still more two years from now. What about five or ten years from now? Inflation, recession, and even economic depression can cause the buying power of your money to drastically decrease. Regardless of the economy, we all still need to eat and feed our families. Food storage is **inflation insurance** which increases your food buying power. Now apply that same wisdom to items such as toilet paper, shampoo, over the counter medicines, and deodorant. Rotating a back stock of sundry items is important too.

Another issue to consider is the quality of the food much of the food offered in super markets is highly processed and full of chemicals and additives. High quality fresh meats and produce has become very expensive. Consider bulk buying at discount stores or joining a cooperative to get the best prices. Gardening, even if it's in containers, can save you a great deal of money. In addition to the savings, fresh picked produce tastes better and has higher nutritional value. Most store-bought tomatoes are picked green and allowed to turn red during processing and shipping. Despite the chemical change that results in a color change, the nutrient content is not the same as vine ripened tomatoes. Key nutrients called phytochemicals depend upon sunlight to form and are lacking in green picked produce. You can create your own back stock of high quality food that you grow or bought with savings from lifestyle changes and smart shopping. This makes food storage **quality insurance**.

Creating your food supply is a very personalized task. Age, activity level, allergies, medical conditions, and personal taste all affect what and how much of it you store. There are many excellent books and websites devoted to the subject of food storage, so I will not try to cover that in depth in this book. With that in mind, the following is a generalized recommendation for one adult's basic needs for one year.

Grains: (mix of types like wheat, rice, spelt, corn, pastas etc.) 400 lbs.
Legumes: (dried beans, lentils, nuts, peanut butter etc.) 60 lbs.
Sugars: (granulated sugar, honey, maple & corn syrups etc.) 60 lbs.
Dairy Products: (canned or powdered milk, powdered cheese, canned or dehydrated butter etc.) 30 lbs.
Fats: (vegetable and nut oils, shortening, canned butter etc.) 30 lbs.
Salt: (iodized table salt, sea salt, bouillon, soy sauce, miso etc.) 6 lbs. for food
Leavening agents: (yeast, baking powder, baking soda, powdered eggs etc.) 6 lbs.

If you are vegan, consult nutrition guides to determine how to adjust your amounts in other areas to compensate for the milk, eggs and cheese recommendation. Similar adjustments must be made by individuals with health problems or food allergies. Remember that these numbers reflect the absolute minimum required for survival. You will not get fat on this diet. It is included to help get people started with the basics to which you can add later.

Whole grain stores much longer than grain processed into meal or flour. Once the shell or outer layer of the kernel is cracked oxidation begins and the aging process starts. As food ages, it loses its' nutritional value. This is also true of many spices such as peppercorns and cinnamon. Wheat, properly stored in a #10 can with an oxygen absorber can last thirty years or more. Once ground into flour, that same wheat in the same can will only last ten years. While this is not to suggest we shouldn't store flours or grain meal, it does mean we should store both and be sure to rotate our food. Another reason to store whole grains is versatility. Dried, whole kernel corn can be soaked to make hominy, coarsely ground to make grits and polenta, and finely ground to make corn meal and flour. Whole wheat can be cooked for a hot cereal, popped for a popcorn like snack, and ground into flour for pastas, bread, and baked goods. Simple adjustments to grain grinders can result in coarse, medium and finely milled grains. These can be used for a variety of purposes. When looking for grain mills and grinders, be sure to buy hand crank models. If there is no electricity, you will still be able to process your grains. Unlike many other products, when it comes to selecting a grain mill – you get what you pay for. There is very little vanity value built into the price. While there are models available for $60-$70, they are smaller, less durable and harder to crank than more expensive models. Table top models with fly wheels are so much easier to turn than those with clamp attachments and hand cranks. $225 is an average price for a good, all metal grinder with decent size hopper. The larger the mill; the more you will pay. Larger hoppers and better handles make grinding easier and faster. Faster is important for large families or groups. Easier is important to older people and those with arthritis and weak or injured arms. Don't forget extra stones to replace the ones that have worn down. Metal options are available for making nut butters from nuts and seeds.

Start by creating a two-week supply and then a 3-month supply of the kinds of food eat daily. This short-term food supply is perfect for "bumps in the road" such as unexpected auto expenses, medical expenses or temporary cut in work hours due to injury or weather. No sense in making things more stressful by changing everyone's diet drastically. In addition to change, long-term packaging is usually much more expensive and thus, a poor choice for short-term use. That said, it is a good idea to help family members become accustomed to long-term storage foods. If you start when they are young, children are very open minded about food. If you missed the boat when your kids were toddlers, there are ways to sneak healthy, thrifty food past a picky eater. With a little effort, you can find recipes even they enjoy. After that is secured, begin adding long-term staples like rice, beans, oatmeal, wheat, dehydrated or freeze dried fruits and vegetables.

Water

The human body is approximately 60% water. To survive, we require adequate hydration. When we become dehydrated, even slightly, we see changes in cognition, muscle function, and strength. Advanced dehydration can cause kidney failure, hallucinations, loss of consciousness, and even death. The physical effects of dehydration occur much faster than those caused by insufficient food. For this reason, it is important to have an adequate supply of clean drinking water.

In addition to drinking water, be sure to have multiple means of filtering bad water. If you catch rain water, take water from a pond or stream, or off a roof, you will need to filter out the chemicals, bacteria, and viruses. Many water-borne substances can result in serious illness or toxicity. Some of the bacteria and parasites found in pond and collected water can result in life threatening diarrhea and debilitating abdominal pain and cramping. Even when there is access to medical treatment, Giardia and Cryptosporidium can cause illnesses that are difficult to recover from. Better safe than sorry. Be sure to have both portable and stationary filters to cover on the go and home base needs. Pre-filtering water through coffee filters or even a bandana or t-shirt will prolong the life of filters by removing the larger particulates.

How Much Water do I Need?

The bare minimum of drinking water is one gallon, per person, per day. High temperatures, exertion, cooking and washing increase this number. Any water can be filtered for safe consumption with the right equipment, but this shortens the life of filters and requires replacement filters. Remember that wash water or garden water can be rain water collected in a 55-gallon barrel from your roof. Boiling it, solar heating, and filtering can make it safe for dishwashing, cleaning, or drinking. Conserve **potable water**, (water which is safe to drink) and reduce filter use, with creative and thrifty methods to pre-filter. Bath water, laundry water, and nongreasy dish washing water can be used to water gardens. If filtered with a low-tech homemade filter system, it can be made suitable for livestock consumption. This water is referred to as **grey water** and can be captured and filtered for secondary use. Don't forget often overlooked sources of water such as water beds, fish tanks, swimming pools, water heater, toilet tank, rain barrels and sturdy plastic trash cans for catching roof run-off.

Uses of stored water

- Drinking
- Rehydrating food
- Cooking
- Washing dishes

- Home sanitation
- Personal hygiene
- Laundry
- Gardening

Containers for Storing Water

Plastic jugs that once held milk or fruit juice are not suitable for storing drinking water. Light weight plastic can retain particles of milk or juice that can taint water, even if you wash it thoroughly. These jugs were not intended for long term storage of potable liquids. Fluctuations in temperatures, especially extreme heat, can cause the plastic to breakdown and become brittle and fail.

There are lots of excellent products for safely storing water available online and in stores. One clever idea we learned of recently for storing water was the use of Mylar box wine bags. These bags, usually purchased by wine making hobbyists, come in a roll and feature an opening for filling and a tap option. You would need to purchase the corresponding size box to store the bags full of water. The big benefit is the portability of these bags. You could put several empty bags in your backpack to capture water. The bags are relatively inexpensive, but the best price is on 1000 count rolls. Consider splitting a roll within your Survival Alliance or with other families who want to be more prepared.

Weight considerations

A gallon of water weighs about eight pounds. With a minimum of one gallon per person, per day, that's fifty-six pounds per week, per person. That adds up fast and can put a tremendous strain on shelving and even floors in mobile homes and multi-story homes. Refer to the manufacturers' specs regarding weight limits. Placing shelves full of water or heavy food or gear against the walls can cause sagging of subflooring if weight limits are exceeded. Don't forget to include the weight of the other furnishings in your calculations. Obviously, homes on concrete foundations do not have these concerns.

When purchasing shelving, pay attention to the weight limit rating on the packaging. Long shelves can sag in the middle if not rated for the load. Metal shelving of the proper strength for the anticipated load or wood shelves on cinder blocks are better than most plastic shelves. Be sure that wood is thick enough and spans are supported with cinder blocks or 2x4 supports for longer spans.

Gear Suggestions

In the event of an emergency, there are certain items that can make life much easier. There are some items like flash lights, candles and matches that everyone would agree are important to have. There are other items, like solar dehydrators, that are wonderful, but a more advanced level item. Such items are useful for long term response to utility disruption or off grid life. Each family and Survival Alliance must decide the degree to which they want to prepare. There are so many products that most of us must prioritize and stick to a budget. Start off with the basics and move down the list. There are many excellent websites and books that can give you product reviews and recommendations. Pinterest.com and Survivalblog.com are treasure troves of free preparedness information.

Clothing Stock Pile

How much clothing you set aside is a personal decision and based on what you are preparing for, space, and budget. At the very least, I recommend having well-chosen clothing and footwear that can be used if you must perform recovery work after a disaster such as a tornado and to keep you warm if you lose power in the winter. Ski bib overalls are easy to find in thrift stores in many areas. They are only worn a few times a year and are often outgrown with little or no wear. The same is true of ski pants and snow suits bought for a vacation trip. While there isn't much choice in color or style, if the power goes out and it's very cold outside, it won't matter to you. Snow jumpers and sleep sacs for babies are also easy to find and much more expensive new. It is better to have them and not need them than need them and not have them, even if they're not your favorite color.

If you are preparing for possible long term hardship, remember to include clothing that is a few sizes smaller than your present size. Hard work and leaner diet will result in weight loss which will make pants sag and shirts hang on you. While fashion isn't exactly important under emergency circumstances, poor fit can cause tripping and catch on things as you work. Undergarments that do not fit can be especially irritating, so consider storing smaller sizes of those items. Belts and suspenders are a must.

Since water and power may be in short supply during an emergency, consider adopting some nineteenth – mid twentieth century practices to stay clean and reduce laundering.

- "Duck baths" can replace daily showers. This involves ½ to 1 gallon of water and a pattern that starts with your face and hair and ends with your privates. For short term outages without running water, consider baby wipes or adult bath sheets to clean up.
- Wear the right clothes for the job. Unless heavily soiled, work shirts and pants can be hung up to air and worn again in a day or two. Sunshine reduces germs and odors.
- Wear an apron, smock or vest to reduce staining and damage to clothing. Wash aprons weekly or as needed for sanitation.
- Scrape shoes and remove before entering the house. Wear "indoor" shoes for warmth. Check for insect or vermin in shoes before putting them back on. Scorpions, spiders, and mice love hiding places. In areas where snakes are found, remember not to put your hands into or under things you have not visually inspected first. Examples are logs, holes, crevices, wood piles and dark corners. After storms, animals, including snakes, can be displaced and find their way into out buildings and even our homes.
- Carry a bandana for wiping your brow and face, not your sleeve.
- Store hats that will provide shade for your face and the back of your neck. Sunburns can be painful, lead to infection and cancer or leave you unable to perform your duties. Hats with chin cinches will help keep it on in windy areas.
- Those with long hair should consider keeping their hair pulled back and braided or in a bun. This prevents tangling and obstruction of vision.
- Keeping hair covered under a hat or pioneer style sun bonnet (for women) will keep it clean longer while providing shade. Patterns for sun bonnets can be found in pioneer or western costume patterns in fabric stores or from historical re-enactor supply sites online. This type of head covering provides a visor to shade the face, a flap or ruffle in back to cover the back of the neck, and ample space to cover braided hair and allow for air flow to cool and shade the head. Covered hair stays clean longer which reduces skin irritation and keeps ticks from dropping on your hair.

Footwear

Proper footwear includes socks and shoes. Caring for these makes them last longer, fit better, and reduces dirt being tracked inside the home or tent. Consider purchasing a heavy- duty boot scraper for your porch. Get in the habit of scraping the soles before coming in and then removing your shoes before entering. Keeping designated indoor shoes or house slippers nearby as well as a place to sit while switching shoes. If this isn't something you wish to do now, remember to set up this arrangement in the event of an emergency. Mud and water from thunderstorms, disasters such as tornados, hurricanes, and the clean-up efforts will be tracked in. In some cases, you may not have electricity or water to spare for clean- up. Frequent changing of socks, airing them between uses, and repairing holes right away reduce laundering needs and extend their life. If the uppers on shoes and boots become muddy, allow them to dry. Then, use a stiff brush to remove the dried mud. Don't forget extra laces.

Entertainment and Special Occasions

Regardless of how we feel about it, society in general, has become dependent on technology for entertainment. If electricity is out for more than a few hours, boredom can become a factor. The younger the individual the sooner this happens and the harder it is for them to entertain themselves. This usually results in behavior problems in children and teens that require the attention of parents or other adults. These adults may have other things they need to attend to. Even adults need diversions to help manage stress and relax. Preparing a box of items that can be enjoyed without electricity is a smart.

When storing supplies that most people may not be familiar with try to remember instructions and patterns. Discount book stores, thrift stores, and garage sales are great places to buy how-to books, patterns, and even supplies for many leisure activities. I've shopped at many garage sales where they were selling yarn left over from various projects, patterns, and needles they no longer needed. I recently bought a brown bag filled with yarn and a stack of patterns for various knitted toys and articles of clothing for $5. Be sure to make multiple copies of the beginner instructions for all activities in your Boredom Buster Box. A ball of yarn can supply enough string for games for a group of people if they all have instructions. Once a few know how to make several shapes or patterns, they can teach others. That one ball of yarn can keep dozens of people entertained for a long time. Additionally, because the loop of yarn can be put in a pocket, it can be readily available to entertain at a moments' notice. Origami, whittling, regular and Chinese jump ropes are all types of frugal, portable and entertaining activities you can prepare for. See the Forms and Check List Section at the end of this book for a list of specific **Boredom Busters** by age.

In addition to entertainment, it is important to plan ahead for special occasions. Despite what else may be happening, we are socialized to mark the passage of time with celebrations. Birthdays, anniversaries, patriotic and religious holidays are an important part of our lives. Acknowledging some of these can reduce stress and lend normalcy to life. Some important occasions to prepare for are:

- Birthdays
- Christenings or baptisms
- Engagements
- Marriage
- New babies
- Deaths
- Religious holidays
- Patriotic holidays

Planning in advance for these events can save time and money now, as well as make them possible under less than ideal circumstances. I developed three things to organize my special occasion preps. First is a **card box** which I filled with cards for various occasions, stationary and stickers. I divided the box by occasion and included gender appropriate cards. Discount stores have an assortment of cards at reasonable prices. When I buy cards for an occasion, I try to pick up one or two for my card box. If I need a card at the last minute, I can go to the box and easily find what I need. In a crisis, I know I can still be thoughtful and make someone feel better on a special day. The second prep I created is a **gift tub** in which I store small gifts. I look for things that just about anyone would enjoy. Good ideas for teens and adults are compact mirrors, brushes and combs, nail care kits, word search or puzzle books, and pocket knives. Gender neutral gifts for young children can include balls, plush toys, coloring book and Crayons, and plastic animal figurines. I add items I know my family would enjoy as I find good deals. When Christmas comes, I have several gifts already. I also include a few items for babies and some hair accessories for girls. These can go a long way toward brightening a child's day. The last idea is a **decoration tub**. In this tub, I collected basic decorations for the most important occasions in our lives. Some occasions will vary, depending on your faith, but most will be the same. Birthdays, engagement announcement/weddings, patriotic observances, and in our case, Easter and Christmas. I am not suggesting full blown decorating, but a few simple things to acknowledge the occasion. If I could not afford to buy decorations or was not able to go to a store for any reason, I could still make the occasion special for that person. Select generic feminine and masculine decorations that can be reused. Avoid characters from television or movies that would date your choices. When selecting what I needed, I was amazed at how little space these items took up.

Simple changes can free up plenty of money to make emergency preparedness purchases. It is never too soon or too late to begin creating your own peace and security and possibly extending that to others. A perfect example is replacing a high price item with an inexpensive item of the same quality and availability. Designer labels or fancy packaging often increase the price without lending added value. Even if you can only afford one extra item with the difference; that is still one extra item you can add to your emergency supply. I found great tasting powdered milk for half what fresh milk costs. I never thought it was possible, but it is. I take the money we normally spend on fresh milk, buy powdered instead, and get something to add to our back stock. If you spend this money on a sale item, it goes even farther. Scratch cooking, staycations, movie rentals instead of theater shows, thrift shop and Craig's List shopping are all great ways to save money for prepping. You can also use your savings to reduce interest bearing debt. This interest is wasted money. If you have credit card balances that carry over or major purchases with loan payments, consider paying extra each month to reduce the principle. Debt is a source of stress and lost income which could be put to better use.

CHAPTER 4
The Survival Alliance Binder

As you work on beginning or increasing your personal and family preparedness, you will come across great articles, websites, recipes and tips. There are many excellent sources of helpful information. The more you learn, the more you realize how much more there is to know. Your bookshelves fill up and before you realize it, you can lose track of what you have and where it is. This is where the Survival Alliance Binder or SAB comes in.

Someone once said, "Knowledge is not power; *Organized* knowledge is power." You can collect tons of information on vital preparedness subjects, but if you can't find what you want when you need it, what good is it? By creating your own SAB you will have the information you need in an emergency at your fingertips. This book teaches a timely method of cooperative preparedness designed to save you from avoidable hardship. After an introduction to the Survival Alliance method of emergency preparedness, we recommend you compile a quick reference notebook of information, divided by topic. There are lots of excellent books on specific topics, but this notebook is designed to be a portable, personalized preparedness guide. We encourage you to collect articles, recipes, lists, and completed Survival Alliance forms. This binder is a great way to keep the most important information at your fingertips which allows training, projects, and weathering an emergency much easier. Imagine how much all your favorite preparedness books weigh. Consider how much information you get from the internet that won't be available without power. Now imagine the best of that information in a one to three-inch binder that you can tuck in a back pack or under a car seat.

Putting it all Together

I recommend buying a sturdy three-ring binder and dividers with tabs. Name each section of your binder. Use plastic page protectors on pages you feel you will use frequently or will be used during projects like canning, outdoor cooking, or foraging. I include a zippered supply pouch to hold pens, pencils, highlighter, a calculator, and small measuring tape. These are nice to have if you need to evacuate to your storm shelter or leave your home unexpectedly. Below are some of the sections you will want to divide your SAB into, but feel free to customize. If you are using purchased index tabs, the titles for each section must be short to fit in the space provided. I made suggestions of short titles and what information can go under that heading. In our first binders, we used a label maker to make small, legible titles and wrote out a full description on the face of the divider page. Of course, how you organize your binder is up to you. The point is to gather the information you will need in an emergency in a concise format. These quick reference pages should be overviews, charts and graphics, and summaries of skills and recipes you will need to succeed after a disaster or crisis of some sort.

Survival Alliance Binder Topic Dividers

- Scouting (SA prospect sheets)
- Roster (Membership and Skill Set Designation)
- Training (Record and Ideas)

- Food (Preparation/Recipes)
- Water (Storage and Purification)
- Medical (First Aid, home nursing etc.)
- Alternative Health (essential oils, herbs, acupressure etc.)
- Shelter (plans, instructions, knot tying...)
- Sanitation (latrines, disease control, insects...)
- Fuels (uses, storage, sources)
- Cooking (methods, cooking tables, substitutions)
- Weather (natural disasters such as tornado, earthquakes...)
- Defense (Self and Home defense techniques, terms, drills)
- Tech/Mech (Technical and Mechanical info)
- Land Nav (land navigation, maps, tracking info)

I also printed helpful or uplifting quotes on the page dividers to help me stay positive. Preparedness often focuses on unpleasant and scary things, so I decided to balance that with some morale boosting thoughts. I included some in the Forms and Checklists section at the end of this book. You can search quotes on various topics online or add your favorite scriptures to your binders. Pinterest.com has great quote suggestions. Another way to use uplifting quotes or thoughts is to make a playing card size deck of them. Punch a hole in the upper left corner and put them on a metal ring with a hinge opening. Use a D ring clip to attach your motivational cards to your backpack or bugout bag. If you find yourself in a situation where you could use a shot of courage or piece, your favorite quotes are close at hand. You can type them on cardstock and laminate them before cutting to size for added durability. **SurvivalAlliances.com** offers an assortment of quotes with various themes on color coordinated cardstock for those who don't have much spare time. Now you have a place for your most important preparedness related information. Have fun filling it up!

CHAPTER 5
Privacy and Security

Before looking for members, it's important to discuss what the military calls OPSEC or operational security. This generally refers to the privacy and information security of a group or mission. When it comes to SA OPSEC the WWII saying, **"Loose lips sinks ships"** applies. It's easy to strike up a conversation with a salesman or cashier and before you realize it share more than you should have. While you may not see the harm in it, unless you are careful not to divulge <u>any</u> personal details, you may have compromised the safety of your group. It's amazing how good the memory of a person can be and how much work they might be willing to put into finding you under the right circumstances.

I recently had an unnerving conversation with an acquaintance at work who is an avid gun owner and very well trained conceal-carrier. I have asked his opinion on firearm related things in the past and we have had many interesting conversations about politics. One day I asked him what his approach to emergency preparedness was. His answer shocked me. He began by explaining that his answer was not directed at me personally, and included the views of many of his friends with similar backgrounds. He went on to explain that he did not have any significant food or other typical supplies stored. He figured that he had more than enough firearms and ammunition to take what he needed. If it came down to it he had no intention of starving, nor did any of his like-minded friends. He further stated that he felt that under collapse circumstances it was survival of the fittest. That was how nature worked; and he felt it was especially true in emergency situations. It is every man for himself in his mind. I have heard this sentiment voiced on websites, in some militia groups and by individuals I strike up conversations with. It is a chilling reminder that there is more to worry about after a disaster than the typical criminal element.

It would be nice if everyone were honest and respected the property of others. Unfortunately, that isn't true on good days, much less when necessities are in short supply. As a Christian, I believe in helping and serving others. What I don't believe in is letting someone steal what I have sacrificed to accumulate for my family. There are generally two schools of thought when it comes to helping and sharing provisions.

1. I have heard folks say, "I'm not sharing with anyone. Most people could have prepared, as I have, but they chose not to. My kids aren't doing without so I can share with people who didn't plan ahead."
2. I also know people who intend to share with anyone who asks for help. "If we suffer because of it, I believe God will bless us for it on the other side."

While I can certainly understand both perspectives, we have chosen to adopt a wait and see attitude. My husband and I pray that we will be inspired to know how to handle situations individually. Sometimes helping will be the right thing to do but, other times it will not. Regardless of which approach you take to the emergency use of your reserves, it is safe to assume that no one wants their preps stolen.

SA OPSEC

Whether you are new to emergency preparedness or not, there are things you can do to decrease the likelihood that you will be the victim of theft or be surprised by uninvited guests during an emergency. This is where **OPSEC** or **operational security** is most important.

Like many things in our lives, the details of your preparedness efforts should remain private. It is helpful to think of these details as you would identity and banking related information. Some information about who you are is fine to share with anyone. Some information you would only share with trusted individuals and other information with only a rare few. In fact, most of the reasons for discretion are the same as those pertaining to identity theft. Advertising possession of things that someone might want to take is dangerous. Giving someone information that is none of their business, can lead to speculation, rumors and awkward encounters. As with all matters of privacy, some folks are more outgoing than others. Before deciding how forthcoming you wish to be, ask yourself how you would respond to breeches of security. Imagine the possible consequences of various preparedness details being shared with outsiders. Are you willing to deal with those issues? This sometimes help clarify the importance of privacy.

Your Preparedness Footprint

Everyone must determine the degree to which they wish to limit others' knowledge of their preparedness measures. I call this your **preparedness footprint**. Like your carbon footprint, which measures the impact you have on the environment, your preparedness footprint is a measure of the information about your prepping activities that is directly traceable to you. How big is your preparedness footprint? How many people, businesses, and agencies know about your prepping? Not everyone shares the same concerns or the same degree of concern. Each family and SA will have to decide what works for them. Many are concerned about **Executive Order 13603**. This order gives the federal government sweeping authority to confiscate property, food, water, fuel, and even conscript you if it deems it necessary during an emergency. I encourage you to read it in its' entirety to decide the impact you feel it has on you and your family. There are allegations of federal phone and email data mining by The Utah Data Center, also known as the Intelligence Community, Comprehensive National Cybersecurity Initiative Data Center. This is the largest data collection and storage facility in the world with the capacity to capture and store historic amounts of data. For those concerned about possible federal government collection of data related to your preparedness activities, consider the following tips:

Reducing your Preparedness Footprint

- Be careful what you research on line. Some topics can raise red flags with Homeland Security. A perfect example is explosives, booby traps, and biological weapons. An occasional article on a website is different than doing research over several days or weeks. If for any reason your computer were searched, research on symptoms of exposure to a dirty bomb or water poisoning might look like "how-to" research. If you do research controversial subjects, keep a log near your computer of topics, dates, and reasons for the inquiries. If you were ever questioned, you would be able to account for your actions. Include home and library searches and book store purchases traceable to you.
- Do not order too many of a specific item at one time. Bulk purchases of items we only use one at a time, and that last for a while, raise suspicion. A case of flashlights, especially high quality ones, screams prepper. Most folks just go to the store and buy another one if one breaks or is lost. Buying large numbers of them looks like you expect not to be able to get them later and are stocking up. Keep large orders of these items to a minimum and spread them out unless you pay cash and pick them up in person. This may mean road trips for the best buy, but it is worth it to many to avoid suspicion.
- Spread your purchases over different vendors or sites. Contact them by mail, when possible. It will take longer, but does not create a data trail the way phone and computers do. Use a money order that you fill out to pay for your purchase. Cashier's checks require you to name the recipient and the issuing institution maintains a record of it.
- Pay cash for books on topics that might be misunderstood. Keep these copies in a discreet location so guests or repairmen won't notice them and get the wrong idea. The last thing you want is the plumber calling the police. He may think he's

doing his patriotic duty to "see something – say something" when you just want to learn how to prepare your family for an active shooter scenario.

- If you call to ask questions of an expert related to easily misunderstood topics, use a pre-paid phone for which you paid cash. Also, pay cash to purchase additional minutes of air time so that the number is never associated with you. This type of phone is good for sending meetings reminder texts for planning conversations. These calls should be made to other prepaid phones. Do not to text addresses of members or training and bugout locations. Consider not making these calls from your home, office or any SA affiliated location. Like computer research, log your calls and the topics discussed. Snail mail is always an option.

- Remember, just because you erased your search history does not mean it cannot be recovered. There are folks that specialize in computer forensics who can ferret out erased or deleted searches, documents, and downloads.

- Pay cash or use reloadable credit cards to pay for in store purchases. Both cannot be traced to you and do not leave a paper trail that can be used to learn what you own. Online purchases must still be mailed and can be traced to you.

Not everyone will feel the need to take all the precautions discussed in this book. I think it is better to have considered the issues than be surprised by an unexpected outcome. Many of us did not consider data mining when we first began prepping. We have been active online and in our communities with groups related to the second amendment, conservative social causes, religious and political affiliations, and shopped 'til we dropped on line for supplies and food. If there is a "list" out there – we're already on it. That said; it's never too late to rein things in a bit, if you'd like to reduce your visibility. Careful consideration, family and Survival Alliance discussion, and prayer can guide you to what is best for you. We all play different roles and are comfortable with different levels of risk. There is no one way to do it, just the way that is best for you.

CHAPTER 6
Survival Alliance Style and Mission

Groups, like people, have distinct personalities or styles. Some groups are laid back while others are all business. Some groups have extensive rules that are strictly enforced and others allow members to self-monitor. This concept of style and mission is based on identity and purpose. This can be observed in sports teams and other recreational pursuits. If you are playing volleyball for fun and the joy of good company, you probably don't want to be on the team whose motto is, "If you aren't playing to win, why play?" It is easy to see how friction could result from the difference between the two perspectives. When talking about Survival Alliances, the need for harmony is even more important. Continuity within the group is essential to smooth functioning of the SA and individual wellbeing.

In addition to your SA style, there is also its' mission. The mission or objective has a great deal of influence on who you recruit, what preps you buy, and how you train. I have spoken to individuals who have grouped together for preparedness purposes and learned that SA missions vary dramatically. Here are some of the group missions:

- Preparing for mainstream concerns such as severe weather, natural disasters, unemployment, illness and injury and the resulting impact on the family/group
- Preparing for economic collapse and governmental over-reach
- Off-grid enthusiasts forming a collective to minimize their dependence on mass produced goods and services
- Preparing for EMP event and the long-term pre-industrial effects on society
- Preparing for economic collapse and resulting hardship and civil unrest
- Preparing for a large range of events connected to Biblical last days prophecy
- Preparing for a large range of events connected to Jewish last days narrative
- Preparing for pandemic outbreak and resulting breakdown in goods and services
- Preparing to respond to shift toward a One World Government
- Preparing for civil breakdown and defense of traditional American values

Many concerns and SA missions overlap or are compatible with other Alliances. We encourage anyone creating or joining a Survival Alliance to network with other groups in your area. Training, bulk buying, ham radio checks, and socializing are great ways to share resources and build good will. While all groups should maintain OPSEC, friendly relationships with other groups can also prove valuable in emergency situations when trustworthy information is needed or bartering could yield much needed supplies or services. Remember that not all collective groups are compatible. There are some that share the same concerns, but are aggressive and opportunistic in their philosophy and mission. Some anarchists and even gangs have adopted preparedness measures, but are criminal in their intentions for survival. Be careful with whom you share information.

When we bought property to develop a self-reliant lifestyle, we named it Stonehaven. The name was exactly what we were building – a refuge or haven for the Stones. After developing a group which included friends, we kept the name because stone also symbolizes strength and permanence. Both words were appropriate for our Survival Alliance. **Naming your group** can provide a unifying feel and instill a sense of pride. Additionally, it provides a way to discreetly identify yourself to other groups. If you are communicating via ham radio, you might say, "Stonehaven and Bugle report that they received no storm damage. Dove sustained minor roof damage to some homes and we have not heard from Chisolm yet." This would give those familiar with these groups valuable information without compromising security. As groups have throughout history, selecting colors, symbols and mottos can galvanize membership around shared beliefs and objectives. These colors or symbols can be used on flags or letterhead to identify communications or messages as legitimate. If you go this route, producing these things now will make them available for use when electricity is not available. If communicating with new members or using couriers, these identifiers can be used to authenticate the communication or vouch for the individual to someone who knows your group name and symbol. Choose designs that are not easily reproduced and store these items in a safe place. Make these items now and store for use during grid down situations.

Another important identifier is the use of passwords. Words or phrases should be developed for use in a variety of situations. Some should be rotated to assure they have not been compromised, while others should remain fixed. We have a family password that is designed for use in instances where the authenticity of a message may be questioned. If critical information is delivered by text, SA member, or stranger, the password assures the recipient that the message is authentic. SA passwords, like computer passwords, should change periodically. Family passwords should remain constant, unless compromised, so youngsters can remember it. Rotating passwords on a schedule helps maintain their effectiveness. Creating a password schedule, well in advance of need, assures that leadership and guards can have printed keys. Consider creating hand signals or gestures that can be used when communicating at a distance. Whether silence is necessary or identification is being made at a distance, identifying signals can be critical. These signals need to be rotated if you suspect that you are being observed.

CHAPTER 7
Creating a Harmonious Alliance

Good Candidates for SA Consideration

There are very few groups in which there are no physical limitations, personality flaws or members who require special consideration or care. When forming a Survival Alliance, try to create a group that is as close to ideal as possible. When recruiting to fill in an existing core group, try to be realistic in your expectations. It is better to have a less than perfect group, than to be without an SA because you couldn't find perfect people. For a Survival Alliance to be successful, **mutual respect** is a must. Individuals who are aggressive, rude or intolerant disturb the harmony of this interdependent team. **Self-discipline** is also an important trait. Members must be able to follow rules and perform their roles, within the group, under circumstances that are physically and emotionally stressful.

Ideally, these individuals should be in good physical shape, and within acceptable weight limits for their height, frame, and age. They should be free of any emotional or psychiatric problems and have a good work ethic. When it comes to those we love, this ideal is not always possible. Despite this, problems can be identified, goals for correction can be set, and plans can be made to deal with these issues. As in life, you make the best of the hand you're dealt.

Which People DO NOT Make Good Survival Allies?

We've all heard the expression, "It takes all kinds to make the world go around." While this is true of society in general, it is not true of Survival Alliances. In the event of an emergency or danger, some personality traits or "kinds" are not helpful to the success of the group. This is not to say that no short comings or differences should exist within an SA. It is nearly impossible to gather a significant number of people perfectly suited to their skill set and to each other. The objective is to avoid choosing members that have behaviors, habits, and philosophies that are obviously in conflict with the group's mission or members in general. Here are a few examples of trouble looking for a place to happen:

- The group you have started identifies primarily as conservative, Christian, and pro-constitution. Frank, a perspective member, has amazing firearms related skill set. He reloads ammunition, is a gunsmith, and an excellent marksman. This would make him a valuable addition to the group. You would like to extend a membership invitation. During the last few meetings Frank has shared that he is not a fan of organized religion and is, in fact, agnostic. Your group makes prayer a regular part of the decision-making process which Frank finds annoying. (**Major philosophical difference**)
- Ellie is the current girl friend of one of the group's communication specialists. While friendly and easy going, she smokes like a freight train. At a pack a day, her smoke breaks are a frequent disruption. The odor is an irritant to some members and also poses a security threat. If she cannot smoke she becomes highly agitated and irritable. (**Addiction issue**)
- Gene and his wife Donna are skilled farmers and ranchers. Gene is very handy with big machinery and no one Dutch oven cooks like Donna. Despite these attributes, both are "know-it-alls". Whenever a problem arises or a decision needs to be made, they feel that their way is best. Much of their input begins with phrases like, "On the farm we...." Or "When I was

_____ I always _____ ....." They try to monopolize discussions and pout if their suggestions are not implemented. (**Control issue**)

- Sid is a man of many talents; an all-around handy man. He is also a heavy drinker. If he's off work, there's a beer in his hand. On the weekend he hits the "hard stuff". Attempts to suggest he cut back have been met with angry outbursts. Sid does not think he has a problem. (**Addiction issue**)
- Carrie and Sharon are inseparable friends. They are both RNs with trauma experience. They are also prone to gossip and seem to stir up trouble in whatever group the join. The most recent problem resulted from the sharing of another group member's confidential conversation. She told Carrie who in turn repeated it. (**Drama Issue**)

While no one is perfect, some individuals have habitual negative traits that can impact your group. If displayed regularly, there's a good chance that it's just who they are. Some individuals are open to constructive criticism and with guidance and patience, can change their behavior. Many cannot or will not change. Careful observation and discernment will help you decide if an individuals' contribution is worth taking a chance on. Here are some of the traits that **are not desirable** in perspective alliance members:

- Argumentative
- Abrasive
- Short tempered
- Excessively critical
- Melodramatic
- Lazy
- Intolerant
- Disrespectful
- sour expression/pouting
- Prone to panic
- Bigoted
- Known gossips and agitators
- Serious substance addictions

Aggressive Disruptors

A Survival Alliance is a collective, communal group whose members may at some point depend upon one another for survival. Individuals who are not good team players or seem to stir up contention disrupt the harmony of the group. These agitators, while they may have valuable skills, jeopardize the group in many ways. If an individual feels he or she is always right, needs to be in charge or is loyal until they disagree with the decision leadership is making, will cause divisions within the group and unnecessary stress.

To decide if an individual personality trait is suitable for your groups' membership, imagine trying to discipline or applying consequence for a violation to this person. Do you see them submitting to the rules and accepting the results of their misstep? This determination is an example of why the vetting process is so important. It cannot be rushed. If not thoroughly and carefully considered, a member can jeopardize the unity and even the physical safety of the group. Here are some situations that illustrate this point:

- You need to gather at your designated retreat location (bug out) and an individual member shows up with additional unauthorized people.
- A member is caught exceeding the rationed amount of food without permission.
- For some, a fight is the answer to most problems. Whether this a verbal or physical fight, those with quick tempers are contentious and often escalate dangerous situations. What if an argument becomes physical?
- An individual who is bossy by nature consistently disregards instructions he is given and does tasks his own way.

- Angry after being disciplined by the group, a member leaves the group and shares details of the SA location and assets with strangers who are willing loot and kill.

These are examples of the many ethical issues that should be considered by the group. Discussions of the various scenarios should be part of group planning. Consensus should be reached as to how these problems should be handled.

Passive / Non-Aggressive Disruptors

Whiners are a drain on the morale and patience of any group. In the event of any emergency there will be hardships. No one wants to be around someone who complains constantly about how hot, cold, hungry, tired or uncomfortable they are. Everyone is in the same boat. Negativity is irritating and makes it hard for others to stay positive.

Individuals who have not developed a strong work ethic or are down-right lazy do not make good SA members. The Pilgrims taught that if you didn't work - you didn't eat. Look for members who are not afraid to get their hands dirty and do what is needed.

CHAPTER 8

Personality Styles and Group Dynamics

There are several general categories that individuals can fall into. The categories or personality styles are a combination of past experiences, skill sets, leadership styles, personal values and ethics. While it is impossible to create a group in which there is never disagreement, it is possible to reduce the frequency and degree of conflict with careful planning.

The broadest categories of individuals are those of **leader** and **follower**. These refer to the natural inclination of an individual to give or receive instruction. While it is tempting to assume that followers are weak, it would be a false assumption. People are most effective when they are functioning within their healthy comfort levels. It is important to identify whether an individual is a leader or follower. Remember that we are discussing things in their broadest terms and about the ideal of each type.

Good leaders are naturally confident and often outgoing. They don't mind the spotlight and often thrive under pressure. They tend to be action oriented. They have good communication skills and are good listeners. Leaders often take a "big picture" approach to problem solving as they lean toward **macro-management**. An individual may be a leader in general terms, but defer to someone else, without hesitation, if they lack the skill set needed. **Micro-management**, as it pertains to leadership style, is generally not well received. This style involves directing every detail of each team member's job. It often discourages creativity, initiative and may be seen as a lack of faith in the team's ability to perform without close supervision. Good leaders know when they are not the best person for the job and will delegate responsibility when necessary. They are comfortable or willing to accept responsibility for their actions and the choices they make. They often have good intuition and tend to follow their "gut feelings". The **best leaders** know they are only as good as those they serve and are humble in their service. They do not lord their authority over those they lead. They lead by example and inspire those they work with. This style is often referred to as the **servant-king** and was best typified by Jesus. Occasionally, you will encounter an Alpha style leader. These are rare and, if humble, is a blessing to the group. Regardless of their tendency toward "top dog" leadership, these individuals must be diplomatic and respectful others.

Followers, on the other hand, do their best work as part of a team. People in this category are most comfortable with specific tasks and excel at their "piece of the puzzle". Many people in this category often excel when they are free to focus on the task at hand, free from the distractions. Once the task is explained, they are set. Followers are generally not comfortable with the spotlight or making decisions under pressure. They usually prefer to take their time and do some research before choosing, making them uncomfortable with clutch decisions. Many followers work well with others and can collaborate to achieve success.

Both leaders and followers are necessary to the success of a Survival Alliance. Despite the value of each style's contribution, it is important to have balance. Everyone cannot be in charge nor can everyone shy away from the tough decisions that must be made. Despite a natural inclination toward one style or the other, many people are flexible and can lead or follow. Use as many of these people as you can to fill out your SA membership. Redundancy, or duplication, in leadership and key skill set areas is vital. If someone is sick, injured or absent, backups will save the day. Consider identifying members within a skill set that can be groomed for future leadership positions or more responsibility. This is good to consider when recruiting. Youth membership is another source of future specialists and leaders. Mentoring and apprenticeship are excellent ways to train interested children and young adults. Working beside family and friends is natural and can be tailored to the attention span and maturity of the student. Young people can even rotate through different skill sets to investigate and discover their match.

When considering your Survival Alliance style, ask yourself the following questions:

- What is the common denominator amongst the group?
- Is there another strong common tie?
- Is this group of people already well trained in their respective skill set or profession?
- Is the group well organized?
- What are the time and economic constraints of members?
- What is the average age of your group members? How many members are children?
- Does your Survival Alliance have property to which they intend to gather for outdoor training and bug out needs? If not, is that a short-term goal?
- Is your membership on the same page politically?
- Do you share similar values and ethical views?

Characteristics that make good Survival Alliance candidates

- Responsible and dependable
- Accepts responsibility for him/herself and actions
- Hard working
- Good social skills
- Tolerant of differences in people
- Aware of current events
- Willing to both lead or follow

Many groups are centered around family. Within a family are all types of people, some of which have less than ideal characteristics and health problems. Our family is a perfect example of this. Like many Americans, my husband and I are working on losing weight to become healthier. A series of car accidents and lifting our son, who uses a wheelchair, have caused me to have back and neck problems. As a result, I have had surgeries to fuse vertebrae in my neck and lower back. One of our sons has a spinal cord birth defect called Spina Bifida. He cannot feel or use his legs and requires assistance with many things. We realize that these facts do not make us ideal candidates for a Survival Alliance. Because of this, we have taken full responsibility for our limitations and have worked to compensate for them. We have gained valuable knowledge and skills to make up for the fact that some of us cannot do hard physical work. We have prepared for our physical needs and sought to reduce the impact our limitations have on the group.

Evaluate your own core group. Whether you are starting or joining a Survival Alliance, be honest about what you bring to the table. These factors will influence the SA you belong to and may require adjustments to membership and preps.

CHAPTER 9

How Many Members Do I Need?

Most people interested in forming a Survival Alliance have people they wish to include from the beginning. This is your **core group** if you are beginning your own SA. These people are most often family, trusted friends and sweethearts. **Reminder - Please read this entire book before discussing your intentions with anyone.** Once you understand the system and the issues involved you will be better equipped to make decisions about who you wish to include in your Survival Alliance.

The most obvious question when considering the formation of an alliance is, "How many people do I need?" Unfortunately, there is not a simple answer to this question. There are many things to consider when determining how many members to have in your SA. Some of the factors that need to be taken into consideration are:

- How big is your core group?
- What are the strengths and limitations of you and your immediate family?
- How well supplied are you in terms of food and gear?
- Do you have enough members to cover the basic needed skills with some overlap?
- How many of your members are children, elderly, or have significant special needs? How many are needed to care for these individuals?
- Does your group have a bug out property?
- How big is the property you need to defend?
- How close are you to neighbors, the city, or major roads?
- What type of property is it - residential, suburban, a farm?
- What kind of topography does the property have?
- How many are needed to post a perimeter guard?
- Are there additional guards needed to cover out buildings?
- How many are needed to cook for your group? How long does each meal take to prepare, plus clean up? Do these people have time to do much else? If there is no electricity, everything will take much longer. Think pioneer era kitchen.

If you already have a bug out location secured, a rough formula might be:

Guard duty roster + replacements + caregivers for the children, elderly, and special needs members = X or the base number of members needed. Now, add appropriate number of cooks and medical personnel and individuals to grow food and raise animals for that number. **X + cooks + ag + medical= estimated number** of people for your Survival Alliance.

Here's how that looks in an illustration:

Bob and Nancy have 4 children. They live a few miles from Bob's parents. Nancy's adult brother, Tracy, lives in town as well. Bob served in the Army with his best friend Ted. Ted is engaged to Cindy. Cindy and Nancy are good friends. This is Bob and Nancy's core group. In a serious emergency, Bob and Nancy have been invited to bring their family to Bob's parents' home outside of town. The property is ten acres and has a well and small pond on it. There are chickens, a horse, and a few head of cattle.

Since the property is fenced and surrounded by neighboring acreage on three sides Bob figures it would only take 3 people to guard the property under normal circumstances using binoculars and walkie-talkies. Night guard duty should be limited to 4 hours, so there needs to be at least two shifts of 3 guards or six adults per night. Bobs' children are 2, 4, 7, and 10 years old. This means at least three of them will require strict supervision and care. At ten years old, the oldest can help babysit, but still lacks the maturity and judgment needed to handle the youngest two alone. An adult will be required to watch the children, but with help from the oldest child, could also serve as a cook or homemaker doing laundry and keeping house. With a core group of 7 adults and 4 children Bob needs a minimum of 4 more adults to cover gardening, cooking and child care. A few more to allow occasional breaks from nightly guard duty and an extra medical specialist would be helpful. This would bring the total to 15 adults and 4 children if none of the new members have young children. Now look at the 15 adults. How many of them can shoot or are willing to learn? Everyone who has guard duty should carry a firearm and be competent with it. With that in mind, 5 of the 7 core group adults are comfortable with firearms. Since Bob's father lives 6 miles from the freeway, Bob decides he needs to recruit ten people who are comfortable with firearms and decent marksmen in case they have unwelcome visitors.

This group now has 19 people; 15 adults and 4 children. A group of 6 share primary night guard duty, with occasional breaks from 4 others. Some of the 4 may be asked to stand guard during the day.

10 guards + 4 children and Bob's mother who is not in good health + 1 adult to watch the children = 16

It will take 2 people to cook for a group of this size three times a day. One person must be the cook and the assistant can share childcare duties with Bob's mother. One person is needed for animal care and 2 designated for gardening and food preservation.

One designated medical specialist (cannot pull guard duty) and one assistant who can be pulled from other duties if needed.

3 agriculture (1 animal care, 2 garden) + 1 full time cook + 2 medical specialists= 6

Bob will need to recruit 1 additional person making the group 20 members.

This is just an example, and so much of this could vary depending upon factors that cannot be known in advance. This is meant to illustrate some of the factors that go into calculating a Survival Alliance size.

Additional variables for consideration include:

- Demographics of your area and that of any bug out location you may have including social, economic, cultural and religious factors
- History of natural disasters such as tornados, hurricanes, or earthquakes
- Behavior of citizens after such disasters and response resources within the area
- Historical examples of political or racial division and resulting problems
- Crime rate and proximity to gangs and organized crime
- Natural resources of area in general and any specific property

A major factor in determining how big your SA needs to be is the type and location of your bug out/fall back location. In a time of upheaval and scarcity of necessities, security will be key to survival. Put bluntly, you will need enough folks with firearms to stand guard to keep criminals from attacking your position and stealing your stuff. You also need to figure in guards who are sleeping and will take over when a shift ends. Guards may have to stand duty 24 hours a day, so divide the day into shifts. Military guard duty shifts range from 4 to 8 hours long depending on the responsibilities of that post. Most criminal activity takes place at night to take advantage of the cover of darkness. If you can, consider shortening night shifts to keep guards fresh and alert. The size of the property will determine how many people you need for guard duty. The types of guards are divided into interior and exterior and stationary and roaming. The topography and vegetation are variables in determining the distance between guards.

Another variable will be the number and type of assets within your property. Examples of assets that may require additional guard are livestock, gardens and fuel storage. These assets are high value targets of the hungry, criminal and even animals such as coyotes or deer in the case of livestock or gardens. Wherever possible, use fencing, solar powered motioned activated lights and alarms to reduce the number of guards needed to guard assets within the property. Take advantage of naturally defensible positions such as hill tops, against hills, or on cliffs.

When it comes to how many you need, the answer is- enough to do what needs doing. Since each SA can be customized, what needs doing will vary.

CHAPTER 10

Scouting for Survival Alliance Members

Understanding the need for discretion, let's look for potential SA members. Initial scouting efforts should consist primarily of observing and listening. Watch for indications of your neighbor's interests. What bumper stickers are on their vehicles? Do you ever see them loading up for weekend or holiday trips? Do they pack camping equipment or have bike racks or RVs? Who do you run into in the outdoor stores, gun range, or sporting goods stores? If you use social media, watch for posts and shared posts that reflect common values and interests. Likewise, note indications of extreme opposition to your values and views. Both types of information can help you decide who you could approach in an emergency.

Possible places to recruit members are:

- Self-defense classes
- Archery shops and clubs
- Gardening, 4H, and FAA clubs
- Preparedness and camping stores
- Gun Shows, gun ranges, and gun clubs
- Organic, vegetarian and vegan lifestyle groups
- Farmer's markets and local food support groups
- Boy Scout of America Packs, Troops, OA and Wood Badge members
- Historic observances such as Civil War re-enactments, LDS Pioneer Day, Land Run observances in Oklahoma or other regional patriotic holiday festivities.
- First responders and related volunteer organizations like CERT or Red Cross

The list goes on and on, but the biggest tip is to look for good people with strong values, who are trainable. Skills can be learned but integrity and a good attitude are either there, or they aren't. These characteristics are the basis for possible shared interests and concern. There are even instances in which you meet someone who has not contemplated preparedness before who becomes the perfect Survival Ally. Sometimes all it takes is connecting the dots between their observations of the world around them and the need for emergency preparedness.

I often feel that sharing that kind of information with someone is a lot like missionary work. The difference is that one saves the body and the other saves the soul. I derive tremendous satisfaction and happiness from teaching people how to prepare themselves and their families for the unexpected moments in life. If you feel like a person is a good fit for your group but they aren't into prepping, don't give up. Consider a fellowshipping approach. Be patient. Some skill set slots are very hard to fill, but it is worth the wait. Even if you aren't successful in "converting" someone, you will have a new friend and will have shared something very important with them.

Survival Alliance Scouting

People watching is a great way to find members for your Survival Alliance. Start with the people closest to you. These are the people you work with, worship with, or the owners and staff at businesses you shop at regularly. You can learn a lot about people by what they do, what they talk about, where they go, what they wear, their shopping habits, and who their friends are. Keeping notes on perspective candidate's helps you to remember which person is which if you are scouting more than one person. As you add more information, a picture will begin forming of that person's character and suitability for your group. **The SA Scouting Sheet** can help you organize your observations to make better decisions. It can be found in **Appendix 1** with the other SA Administrative forms. Remember; **never violate anyone's privacy or trespass** as you learn more about them.

The **SA Skill Survey** is a good tool for learning what your members know and what they want to learn more about. Combined with the **SA Skill Group Roster**, you can track how many members you have with each skill and their level of skill. You can also keep track of who has interest in which skills so you can look for training opportunities in that area. The Skill Survey can also help identify gaps in your SA so you can recruit effectively.

Conversation Starters

Finding potential members to fill out your Survival Alliance is a simple matter of observation and conversation. The process of identifying possible members and starting prepping related conversation is a lot like sharing your faith. The best approach to sharing something that has blessed your life and can be good for others is to fellowship. Here's how this approach works:

1. Get to know those around you. Your neighbors, co-workers, staff at businesses you frequent, and organizations to which you belong such as church, gym, or scouts. PTAs are also great places to start if you have kids. You have common interests within these settings, so it's easy to strike up a conversation.

2. Service is a wonderful way to interact with friends and neighbors. Not only is it a source of good will, but it provides opportunities to learn about one another. The conversations you strike up as you rake leaves, pull weeds, drop off a batch of cookies or help paint the walls of a nursery can help you get to know and understand others.

3. Discussing current events such as politics, the economy, weather, education or crime rates provide opportunities to discover the thoughts and opinions of others. Without being overbearing, share your thoughts and opinions on the topics that come up. Remember their opinions may differ from your own, so be respectful. These exchanges of thought and opinion will help you identify who shares similar views and values.

4. Drop bread crumbs of information and see who follows your trail. Just like feeding ducks at the park, drop pieces of bread, not slices. Comments like," The kids and I have to be up at the church to leave for scout camp at 5 am." or "I'm heading to Bob's Bait and Tackle across town. Do you need anything while I'm there?" Comments and questions like these let you share a bit of what you do and invite a response from the listener. If they share interests, conversation will flow naturally. You might even sense a type of chemistry between you or your families. Be careful not to over share though. Many may not indicate interest and that's ok. You have both learned more about one another. If there is an emergency in the future, you now know a little more about that person. This information can be helpful in organizing neighborhood or community assistance. If they respond with questions or indicate similar interests, you can pursue the conversation further. Keep notes on what you learn about others. **The SA Scouting Sheet** can help you keep up with what you learn. This will help you identify individuals that you may be able to work with on emergency preparedness. It can also serve as a resource in an emergency or disaster to help organize, help, and manage problems. Too much information can result in overwhelming the uninformed or inexperienced or tipping your hand to someone who may not share your values. In an emergency, this can come back to haunt you.

5. Once you have spent time getting to know people, some will stand out as having similar values and opinions as you and your family/group. Deciding which ones might be interested in preparedness on a group or alliance level is a gut decision. While there is risk involved, it is worth it. Remember, nothing ventured - nothing gained.

6. After you have identified a potential source of shared interest or indication of shared values, use this to start a conversation. If you see a bike rack on the car, ask a question like, "Who rides?" or "What do you ride?" to start a conversation. Common ground allows for further interaction. More interaction allows opportunities for further discovery and understanding.

Using a dating analogy, remember that not all prospective candidates will turn out to be one you "take home to meet mother". Despite this, do not get discouraged. The right ones are worth waiting for. Take your time, put effort into your observations and interactions, and be prayerful about your selections. It is a good idea to invite others in your family or group to spend time with candidates on your short list for inclusion. Choose activities that will test character traits such as stamina, temperament, teamwork or knowledge. A single outing is not enough, any more than a single date would be a wise basis for choosing a spouse. Multiple outings with different people, doing different things will give you a much better picture of who they are. Remember that these individuals are not fully vetted, so no last names or indications of who is in your group. Just introduce them to members something like: Dave, my friend from work or Cindy, my gardening partner at the community garden plot.

CHAPTER 11
The Vetting Process

At a certain point, you will discover if there is chemistry or significant common ground with a prospective candidate. Conversation can then evolve into topics more specific to your preparedness interests. Although there are no guarantees, your gut instinct is usually right about folks at this point. It is important to adhere to the rules your SA has established for information sharing and introduction of prospective members. Mutual trust is critical to group harmony and should be honored.

Vetting Tips

The vetting process for an SA is a lot like dating with the objective of marriage. At first casual dating helps you find candidates you have things in common with. Later, the list shortens and the activities become more personal. It is important not to rush things. You would never say "Hi. My name is Bob. Do you like to ski? Me too. I love you. Let's get married." We generally exchange information about ourselves in an "I'll show you mine if you show me yours" sort of way. If the other person does not react favorably to something that you put out there, we generally pull back, wait and try again later. If it is still not received well or reciprocated, we make the mental note that that road is a dead end. This sometimes ends the relationship or at least the notion of marriage. Despite this, that individual may remain a trusted friend and confidant, just not a spouse. Apply this to vetting a potential SA member, remember that **once you share information it cannot be taken back**. If a person doesn't seem ready to make the leap from generally aware and prepared to prepper, don't give up. People who are trustworthy and of good moral fiber could be considered in layaway. In the event of a disaster, they can be called upon for assistance. Since you have gotten to know them well, it will be easier to work together. Keep their SA Scouting Sheet and mark them as appropriate for general emergency response. Others will prove to be excellent matches and the topic of communal preparedness can be broached.

Topics under this heading include:

- Sharing bulk food purchases and re-packaging together
- Canning or dehydrating together
- Taking a class together on a preparedness topic
- Organizing a bulk item purchase to receive a discount or free shipping
- Joint family camping, hiking or other outdoor activities
- Monthly shared meals cooked without electricity

All these activities are useful skills to develop. As you share these skills with others they grow in their skill level and confidence in their abilities. Over time this may lead to a shift in their feelings making them approachable as SA members. Again, trust your gut.

Back to the dating analogy; don't forget to tap resources such as those who are already SA members. It's like asking a friend if they can fix you up with one of their friends. Like-minded folks have friends you may click with. Maybe they will be a good match for your Survival Alliance. Third party introductions can serve as a screening process. Like many exclusive clubs, you must know someone to get in. This helps weed out pretenders and worse, moles, who can jeopardize the safety and well-being of your group.

Some groups may wish to be more formal in their vetting of potential members. Asking for letters of introduction, character references, and back ground checks are all ways to learn more about the trustworthiness of an individual. Many organizations, such as the Boy Scouts of America, require volunteers to submit to background checks to reduce possible fraud and danger to the youth they serve. Many feel if you do not have a criminal past you should not object to submitting to a background check. Occasionally, you may have an applicant who has misdemeanor charges from their college days. Some may even have a checkered past from which they have reformed. These revelations may not be common knowledge, even within their family and may be a source of considerable embarrassment. It is wise to limit who sees these reports and treat this information with the same respect and courtesy you would want in their position. Consider shredding these and any other sensitive information as soon as it has served its' purpose.

In the end, it will still come back to a gut decision. Background checks are helpful, but not foolproof. A clean record may only mean you have never been caught doing something illegal and not all forms of dishonesty are a crime. The best indication of whether you can trust someone is a combination of as many methods as possible and time. Only time will tell if you have chosen wisely.

CHAPTER 12
Candidate Physical & Mental Fitness

Assessing Limitations

n an ideal world, everyone would be healthy, athletic and able to tackle any activity with ease. We would have SAs made up of world class athletes and even our senior members would have enviable stamina. Unfortunately, the truth is far from this ideal.

Many families, like ours, have a member or members, with some type physical limitations. When forming a Survival Alliance, we must accommodate our family members and even our own physical limitations or disabilities and find ways to prepare with that in mind. Those with physical limitations can find meaningful ways to contribute to the wellbeing of the group. Don't automatically discount them, or yourself, because of age or physical limitation. Their wisdom and skills can still make them a valuable member of your SA. Those who are lazy will either do a poor job of the work they are given or shirk their responsibility altogether. Remember that the safety and wellbeing of others rests on the integrity of tasks done by everyone on the group.

Substance addiction, regardless of its' form, is not conducive to SA membership. If an individual is a heavy drinker, smoker or abuses prescription or street drugs they cannot be counted on. In the event their supply runs out they will suffer physically and emotionally. Some of these symptoms are not only a problem for them, but spill over to the group. Erratic, violent, and deceitful behavior is not uncommon in those going through withdrawal from addictive substances. An individual may even betray the safety of the group for the promise of relief and a fix. Those who smoke or have caffeine dependency are encouraged to wean off these substances to assure peak performance in a time of crisis.

Those who are flighty or panic easily are not dependable under stress. They are a distraction because they require the assistance of other group members to regain their composure. If overcome by stress or fear, they may not be able to perform their assigned duties. This places an undue burden on other members who must take up the slack. It is important to ascertain the cause of the flightiness. Is this an individual lacking skills and thus, is anxious? If so, Ignorance can be corrected. With training, anxiety can be replaced by competency and self-esteem. In other instances, this behavior can be the result of character flaws or mental health issues. These causes are much more difficult to address and are usually outside the skill of non-professionals. I am referring to individuals that are excitable and overwhelmed easily by temperament, not those with developmental disabilities. Avoid recruiting those who cannot remain calm under stress.

Mental Health Conditions

Some individuals suffer from mental health conditions such as panic attacks, depression, bi-polar disorder or PTSD. They may take prescription medication. For some, medications help them lead a normal life, much like those with high blood pressure or high cholesterol. For others, medication does not completely address the emotional problems they struggle with. Remember that in a long-term hardship, medication will not available. Individuals who are dependent on medication for mental health, like any medication, are encouraged to try to build a back stock and alternatives methods of treating their condition. If there are members with such conditions, have them share how the group can assist them should medication be unavailable. Individuals who will become emotionally unstable to the point of being dangerous, to themselves and others, require special screening. Schizophrenic or psychotic behavior can be dangerous and unpredictable and may require the individual to be restrained or confined for safety purposes. Your

SA will need to decide if that is something they are prepared to do and plan accordingly if choosing to admit individuals with serious mental health condition.

Please don't misunderstand and think that I am discriminating or that I am suggesting these individuals be excluded from our preparedness plans. We have a child who is bi-polar and group members who are adults with ADD. I know from firsthand experience some of the issues that mental health problems bring. Families and groups dealing with these issues must strive to mitigate as many of the problems as possible. This is also true of any physical ailment or limitation.

Physical Health Conditions

Almost everyone has room to improve physically; whether it's losing some weight, lowering our cholesterol, or being in better shape. Here are some health issues to consider when forming Survival Alliances.

Constitutional Strength

Some people are very sensitive to heat or cold. These people are easy to spot if you spend much time with them. They are always hot or cold when everyone else feels fine. They frequently adjust the thermostat, vents in the car or sit out of activities because they are too hot or cold. The most difficult to deal with is heat sensitivity. While few people want to be hot or sweaty, some cannot tolerate it without becoming ill. This is a constitutional issue and is rarely within the control of the individual. These folks are often red faced with the slightest outdoor exertion.

When selecting SA member, look for individuals that seem to tolerate heat within normal parameters. Heat sensitive individuals who are SA members should be given responsibilities that keep them out of the sun and do work in early morning or at night.

Some individuals have health conditions that make exerting themselves difficult or impossible. In this case, we are referring to general constitutional weakness. With the exception of heat sensitivity, many who tire easily are simply soft and out of shape. Opportunities should be found to work alongside potential SA members to determine their stamina. Individuals that simply need to increase their endurance can be helped to do so in a friendly, supportive way. The key to success is whether they see the wisdom in changing their fitness level as an indicator of commitment to the group.

Orthopedic Problems

There are many types of problems that involve the bones and joints which can impact your SA. Old injuries that have left a limb prone to re-injury, wounds that did not heal properly, malformations, various types of arthritis, back problems and plantar fasciitis are some examples. The two biggest areas of concern are the ability to walk and carry more than a few pounds. In an emergency, the ability to do both can be very important. While orthopedic limitations need not be a deal breaker, extra thought and planning must be done to be sure everyone's needs are met. It is also important for those individuals to have the equipment or supplies needed to treat or compensate for their injuries or conditions. If they require assistance be sure that there are still enough members to do the other jobs required and allow for a few extra ill or injured.

Obesity

While not actually a disease itself, clinical obesity is the cause of many serious health conditions such as heart disease and high blood pressure. This is not new information to most of us, but what isn't discussed in public service ads, medication or diet aid commercial or in the gym are the more personal effects. These side effects are often the private struggles of the seriously overweight and can have big impact on their performance within a SA. Some problems are the results of over-burdened joints which ache or become worn and require bracing or surgical intervention. Walking long distances and strenuous exercise can tax the frames of overweight individuals who are already carrying an extra burden. Another problem not often discussed is skin breakdown in the folds and creases of the skin. Heat, moisture, and friction combine to cause irritation. These conditions can lead to chaffing, blisters, yeast infections and decubitus ulcers. Left unchecked, the resulting pain and infection can be debilitating and dangerous. Hemorrhoids, podiatric problems and gastric reflux are also common complications of being seriously overweight. If you are considering, have or are an obese individual, make sure to take these limitations into account. Build a back stock of products to address common ailments and be especially watchful for early signs of distress. Encourage and support overweight candidates to become healthier.

Other Health Concerns

There is a very long list of health problems an individual can have. Some are the result of injury; while others are the result of disease. Diseases that damage the vital organs such as the heart, lungs, kidneys, pancreas, or liver are especially dangerous as they usually require expensive prescription medication. Without these drugs, many people will not survive long. For this reason, it is important to carefully prepare a back stock of medication and alternative methods of treatment where possible. Refilling prescriptions as soon as they are eligible for refill can result in a few extra doses over time. Anything is better than nothing. Research alternative treatments that do not require a prescription.

Talk to your doctor or pharmacist about any symptoms caused by not taking your medication. Some have serious side effects if they are stopped suddenly. Learn if there is a weaning off protocol you could follow if it were obvious you would run out before you could restock. If you have discovered alternative treatments you feel comfortable with, you could begin them as you stop your prescription medication.

- Be sure that all critical responsibilities assigned to individuals with serious health problems can be performed by others within the group.
- Educate the group about the strengths and weaknesses of members with health problems. All members should be able to recognize and know how to render aid for events such as heart attack, stroke, seizures and diabetic issues such as high and low blood sugar.
- When conducting drills, include likely medical emergencies and practice the appropriate response. Consider makeup and props to simulate injuries.
- Anticipate realistic progression of health conditions of a candidate or members within the group and be sure that needed supplies and equipment are included in preparations.
- Individual and collective stores of braces and splints for various body parts are important for accidents and injuries. There are many places on line and in newspapers to find used durable medical equipment at huge savings. Wheelchairs, walkers, crutches, canes, and bedside commodes can also be found at thrift stores and garage sales. Be sure to wash and sanitize all equipment before storing. Most of these are generic or come in pediatric and adult small, medium, and large sizes. Look for a variety of sizes and store in plastic bins with lids labels. Keep an inventory of what you have and a list of what you still need. Put a list of what you still need in the glovebox of your car. If you decide to go to garage sales, you have a reminder list of things to look for.
- Learn home nursing skills. If there were an outbreak of serious flu or epidemic of a debilitating disease, knowing how to care for someone at home would be a valuable skill. Be sure that a few people per household learn these skills. Needed skills include occupied bed change, bed bath, preventing pressure sores and skin break down, dealing with pathogens carried in blood, body fluids, or in the air, and nutrition for healing. These skills are taught as part of the CNA (certified nursing assistant) course offered at many vo-tech schools. The study materials can be purchased in their school bookstore or online. Some include videos that demonstrate various techniques such as transfers.
- Consider having one person take a CNA course and train interested members of the group. There are many places to take this course and successful completion results in a certification that is often recognized in multiple states. You never know when the job skill may be needed.

Overall, mental and physical fitness is extremely important to emergency preparedness. Whether you are working on stress reduction or weight loss, remember to shoot for lifestyle changes instead of gimmicks and quick fixes. Learning ways to deal with any health problem you have can sometimes be difficult. Don't be discouraged if a method you try doesn't work. There are many ways to deal with most issues. Hang in there until you find ones that work for you. If you are working with family or other SA members, be supportive and patient. Share resources that may be helpful and offer to work with them on fitness goals if they would like. In the end, your Alliance will be better for it.

CHAPTER 13

Possible Membership Requirements

Provisional Membership

We have discussed traits and factors to consider when choosing potential members for a Survival Alliance, but what next? To maintain security, order and a sense of fair play, and provide for the needs of all members, it is important to have some basic admission requirements. All members must meet the selected requirements to join the Survival Alliance. An individual's commitment to preparedness and the group can be tested and trust earned as they complete the admission requirements. Applicants can be given graduated access to the SA. As they meet incremental requirements for food, gear and skills they can be granted additional access and privileges.

During this initial period, candidates are provisional members. **Limiting information** such as exact location of bug out retreat, member addresses and last names, and details of the alliance defensive capacity protects the group until the candidate has graduated to full membership. Should the applicant fail to fulfill their obligations or change their mind they have not had access to the most sensitive information.

General Requirements

Asking all members to bring the same basics to the group creates a level playing field. Consider creating a basic list that everyone is expected to acquire, regardless of their skills. The specific details of the requirements will depend on what type of Survival Alliance you have. There are many possible additions to the basic lists below. Additional requirements vary from group to group based type and style. A para military style group will be heavier on the firearm and ammo requirements as well as LEO or military focused skill sets. This could also include style specific vernacular, dress, and equipment. Some faith based Survival Alliances may require specific religious affiliation, congregational membership, as well as scripture study and prayer as part of all meetings. Some groups are centered on political ideology. Membership in the group may be based on party affiliation, activist work, and candidate support in addition to the standard preparedness requirements.

Be sensitive to the financial limitations of some candidates and members. Be flexible, creative and supportive as they work toward their admission requirements. Check with candidates regularly and offer moral support and ideas for fulfilling their goals. Occasionally, a member may be making good progress but may have circumstances arise that make them unable to reach a goal by their deadline. Consider granting a formal extension of the deadline. Adding a formal extension to their initial entry contract provides documentation in the event of a change in SA leadership. It will also provide a record of the extension for future reference.

From this it is easy to see that there are many different types and styles of groups. It is critical to find or create a group that best represents your beliefs, degree of commitment to training, and prep acquisition. There are many things that you could ask a candidate to have, do, or be. The list you chose will reflect the style of group you have. Some SAs are very formal in their structure and have strict admission requirements. Others are less regimented and have flexible admission requirements. Regardless of how many requirements there are or how strict these prerequisites to membership are, they generally fall into 6 categories.

1. Food
2. Water

3. Gear
4. Skills
5. Philosophy
6. Attachment/relationship.

Food and Water Requirements

As we all need it to survive, food and water should be the first and most important requirement. The amount and type vary from one group or SA to another. The most common specification for food is a one year supply per person admitted. This can seem like a daunting goal, but there are many thrifty and clever ways to build this amount of food. Some require all 12 months up front while others ask for 3 months upon admission to the group and allow members to work on acquiring the rest over time. If you go with the latter, consider quarterly goals toward that end. Institute an opportunity to review each member's progress, answer questions, and encourage them toward their goals. There are many books, websites, and blogs dedicated to the acquisition of food and water storage so I will not cover the subject in depth. I would suggest that individuals adjust their mindset from a years' worth of the food you eat now to basic staples that will sustain life. Especially when purchased in bulk, or at an LDS Home Storage Center, these staples are surprisingly affordable. It is a matter of prioritizing how money is spent.

General Gear Requirements (backpack or other example of gear)

What gear you require will depend upon the types of events your group is preparing for. Those who are focused on weather and other natural events may not be interested in the same gear as those concerned about an EMP. Despite the spectrum of concerns, the following are good suggestions for all groups:

Basic Gear Requirements

- Family size first aid kit
- Commercial grade can opener (for #10 cans)
- Heavy and light duty work gloves
- Chainsaw, chain oil, fuel additive and fuel
- Sturdy backpack with ample storage and external pockets for go-bag
- 72- hour kit - basic supplies and food for 72 hours – see list
- High top work or hiking boot – gives ankle support and sole protection
- Water filter (personal and a family size)
- Assorted knives; self-defense, utility, field dressing game and cleaning fish
- Sharpening stone, oil, and scabbard for fixed blade knives.
- Firearm, ammo and cleaning kit where permissible and desired
- Rechargeable/ solar powered lanterns
- Hand crank powered transistor and weather radio
- Battery powered and rechargeable flashlight
- solar chargers for personal devices, lanterns and radio
- tent large enough for household or 2 or 3 smaller tents for big family

Mechanical / Technical Requirements

During emergencies, a good set of tools and a well-chosen stock of hardware, products and equipment for maintaining and repairing things are essential. If you're handy, you can repair or make things needed to cope with the problems that arise. Even if you aren't that handy, having the right tools for the job can enable you to get help from someone who is. If you have the supplies to make the repair, you could barter for what you need.

- Adjustable crescent wrench
- Standard set of sockets and wrenches
- Metric set of sockets and wrenches
- Set of standard wrenches
- Set of metric wrenches
- Set of screwdrivers in multiple sizes and types
- Allen wrench set, preferably in folding style
- Hammers – consider ergonomic composite handles
- Hand saws for lumber and cutting branches and logs
- Hacksaws with replacement blades for various materials
- Wide selection of nails, screws, nuts and bolts
- Reference manuals/trouble shooting guide for vital equipment
- Bolt cutters for cutting chains/ pad locks if keys are lost or access to an area is required in an emergency
- Rotary hand drill which can be found cheaply at garage and estate sales are invaluable. Don't forget bits in various sizes.
- Carpenter's planer for making logs into flat boards. They are available at hardware stores as well as yard sales inexpensively.
- Electrical wire of various capacities and purposes as well as wire cutters and strippers.
- Soldering gun and supplies (to be run off a generator)

Again, there are extensive lists of gear on many reputable sites and in some excellent books that you can refer to create your requirements list. The important point to take away from this is the need to be specific. Supplies members should acquire and time frames by which they should have them should be outlined in the membership contract. Written checklists and opportunities to inspect purchases will help provide accountability. Stress the interdependence of all members and provide positive re-enforcement for reaching goals.

Secondary goals are a good way to help members faced with a large number of requirements. Groups who are also concerned about events with long-term effects on the economy and the ability to purchase new gear, can expand on the first list of requirements. These additional items are non-food supplies that would cause hardship if you ran out, lost or broke them. Secondary goal items can be part of a second list of requirements for individuals who are already members. These **follow-up goals** can help defray the cost of initial acceptance and serve to test the commitment of the new member to gaining full access membership. If you go with a staggered set of requirements, remember to withhold full access to sensitive information. If a member has not met all requirements, they should not know the exact location of your bug out property or names of all SA members. Defensive plans should also be withheld until members have completed all requirements. This list is not comprehensive, but is a representation of the type of things you should consider.

- Advanced medical supply kit (geared for times when no doctor is available)
- High performance thermal under wear (moisture wicking, quick drying)
- Quality rain gear (hooded jacket and pants and rain boots)
- Large solar charger for recharging batteries and running small appliances (We like Goal Zero)
- Firewood - _____ cords with tarps and bungee cords to cover them
- Gasoline and/or diesel _____ gallons in approved 5 gallons cans
- Specific amounts of automotive fluids
- HAM radio set up and one Technician level certified person per household
- Bicycle for each member of household (flat proof tires or replacement inner tubes, tires, and pump)
- **Clothing and Gear Repair Kit – App 2**

Skill Requirements

All the food and gear in the world won't help much if people don't know how to use it. Skills are necessary to utilize the equipment properly and make best use of the food and water stores. In selecting perspective SA members, it is important to have a wide range of skills and built in redundancy. If the only person with a vital skill becomes ill or is not available, the group suffers. We suggest a list of basic, **entry level skills** that all members 16 and up should have. A few in each group are all that are needed for other skills. Like food and gear, not all skills can be acquired at once. It is a smart practice to set up learning opportunities so that members can refresh or learn new skills. Ongoing education is critical to smooth group performance. Set goals with dates for acquiring specific goals and follow up to see how things are going. To build trust and a sense of community, share the progress members are making during regular SA meetings. This will instill a sense of confidence on the part of individuals and trust within the group.

Entry Level Skill Suggestions

- Basic First Aid
- CPR/AED use
- Knife safety
- Fire starting
- Basic knot tying
- Firearm safety
- Water purification
- Various ways to collect water
- Packing a backpack
- Identify Poison Ivy and Sumac
- Determining direction in nature
- Low impact camping practices
- Military hand signals – top 5-10
- Know how to operate all your gear
- Personal hygiene and sanitation
- Transportation of ill or injured
- Basic direction finding – orientation

Intermediate Level Skills

- Advanced first aid
- Building search protocol
- Cribbing and extrication
- Firearm maintenance
- Firearm marksmanship
- Cooking without electricity
- Basic gardening and sprouting
- Orienteering and land navigation

Advanced or Expert Level Skills

Skills beyond Intermediate become more suitable to specialization. These skills should be developed by individuals who have both aptitude and the fitness level required. Remember to have multiple people able to perform crucial tasks, even if it is not their primary responsibility. When considering individuals for a Survival Alliance, look for folks who already have some skills but also show aptitude to be taught other important responsibilities. Even if a candidate does not currently have a specific skill, you can ask them if they would be willing to learn. Commitment to master a skill is a great way to fill gaps in a group's collective skill set. This commitment should be formalized in a contract with specified dates for review of progress and evaluation of progress. As mentioned before, individual and group recognition is important to morale and team building. Don't forget the value of a phone call or text to check on a member's progress. Encourage new members by asking how a class or course they took went. Acknowledgement of progress, completion of goals and the willingness to take on new responsibilities should take place during SA meetings. Sharing these milestones builds unity and confidence within the group. Additionally, acknowledgement of the effort and financial commitment involved assures members that they are valued and appreciated.

Remember that many of these requirements can be pricey. Be considerate of the budgets of provisional members. While these items are important, relationships are too. Economic stress can cause family and group stress which is not good for the Survival Alliance.

CHAPTER 14
The Seven Skill Sets

A Survival Alliance requires **seven basic categories of skills** to be successful. Within these categories are numerous specific jobs or specialties. It is important to have duplicates of the more important skills. This is especially true of critical skills such as medical and defense. While this list is not all inclusive, it is a good start to growing out your Survival Alliance. Your specific geographic location may require skills not listed. Customize your sub-skill list to reflect any factors unique to your area. The **Skill Groups** are:

- **Medical**
- **Defense/Security**
- **Agricultural**
- **Mechanical/Technical**
- **Food Preparation and Preservation**
- **Morale (mental and spiritual health, also responsible for arranging training)**
- **Special Care (babies, children, expectant women, elders, those with disabilities)**

When determining the number of people needed to run a successful SA, calculate how many people one individual can serve in an acceptable period of time. An example is **Food Production and Preservation**. How many people are needed to cook for the number of people in the group – three times a day? Include clean up. Remember that this will most likely be done under less than ideal or even pioneer era conditions, so everything will take longer. Also, remember that some individuals can have overlapping responsibilities. Develop a list of tools and equipment needed to do communal cooking. Remember that meal prep will most likely happen without the use of electricity. Acquire needed items and maintain appropriate levels individually and at the SA level. Instead of every household having everything, consider making a list of the big ticket or seldom used items that can be shared within the Alliance. Members can pitch in to buy some items that are owned collectively or assignments for equitable purchases can be made. Individuals with corresponding specialty skills are logical choices for these assignments. Either method can increase inventory quicker and for less money than getting these same items in every home. An example within our Alliance is a tooth extraction kit. These tools are pricey and you don't need one in each family. This equipment was bought by our RN.

Be sure to keep records of who bought what, how much it cost, and where it is being stored. Each SA will need to establish policies for maintenance and repair of such equipment. Decide what happens if a member who made a communal purchase leaves the Alliance?

Skill Group Job Descriptions
Medical

Under the heading of medical is a long list of skills that are needed within the group. Some skills should be left to trained professionals, others to specialists, and still others should be learned by all. First aid is a commonly needed skill.

Level 1 skills for <u>all group members</u>:

- Basic first aid
- CPR / AED
- Recognize the signs of stroke and heart attack
- Basic bandaging and splinting
- Hygiene and disease prevention

Level 2 skills Suggested for Medical SG specialists

- All skills on the list above
- Wound care and infection control
- Fingernail and foot care – damage prevention and treatment
- Laceration closure – medical glue, stitches, and staples
- Use of herbal and natural alternative health care techniques and remedies
- Home nursing skills – bed bath, occupied bed change, pressure relief, communicable disease management, nutrition for healing…

Level 3 skills Suggested for Experts such as nurses, doctors, dentists, chiropractors

- Identification of specific diseases and bacteria
- Determination of the correct medication to treat pain and infection
- Splinting and setting broken bones and dislocations
- Treat gunshot wounds, crush injuries, and amputation
- Understanding various mental health conditions/ medications
- Dental work such as extractions

Security and Defense Skill Group

This skill set encompasses all the tasks and procedures that keep members' information and their possessions safe from harm. This harm could be a breach of personal information, wandering eyes that notice the content of your food storage room or the theft of a generator. **The Security and Defense Skill Set** is responsible for the creation and implementation of measures that mitigate harm to the Survival Alliance and a response to any breach of security. These are further broken down into **threat prevention** and **threat response** categories.

Threat Prevention

- Document security – proper storage of all sensitive information related to the Survival Alliance and its members.
- Locks, keys, combinations to pad locks and safes, entry codes, passwords, coded communications, computer safety, and other forms of limiting access.
- Planning evacuation routes and alternate routes during inclement weather
- Designing camouflage for locations, equipment, and individuals
- Creating appropriate caches of basic and defensive materials

- Testing security measures and drilling procedures as needed
- Coordinating with SA leader to determine and issue alert status

Threat Response

- Making recommendations in response to alert status changes
- Securing agreed upon quantities of specified ammunition for all firearms
- Maintaining all firearms within armory and replacement parts
- Maintaining reloading equipment and supplies
- Securing and maintaining supplies, parts, and arrows/bolts for all bow types
- Conducting or arranging firearms training
- Developing plans for dealing with trespassers (before and during emergency)
- Active shooter response planning and group training (public and SA locations)
- Develop plans for responding to riots, gangs, and unlawful use of LEO/military
- Issue COA (course of action) for specific threats, to direct the group in situations not anticipated or prepared for in advance.
- Make strategic recommendations to the SA leader
- Creation of guard schedule and roster for specified drills and during emergencies

Agriculture Skill Group

This Skill Set Group is tasked with the responsibility to provide fresh food for the group. This responsibility can begin now and provide food for canning and dehydrating or to supplement member's daily meals, thus freeing up money for SA purchases. If this option is chosen, members may be asked to purchase canning supplies, seeds, or chip in for additional water usage where well water is not available in exchange for their share of the produce. If farm animals are being raised for meat or milk, members may be asked to share in feed costs or the purchase of starter animals. If these responsibilities do not begin until an emergency or evacuation order is issued, members may be asked to chip in to pay for a seed and feed stockpile for use at that time. Hunting, fishing and trapping fall under this Skill Set Group.

- Become knowledgeable about crops that grow well in your area as well as any bug out location including times for planting, weather related information pertaining to raising crops and animals, pest control and harvesting timetables.
- Knowledge of animals raised for food as well as animals used for riding or pulling. This includes feeding, watering, illnesses and injury care, preventative medicine, horn and hoof maintenance, dental and coat care, pregnancy, delivery, and newborn care.
- Plans for or creation of proper housing for animals and seasonal preparations
- Creation of feed stock pile, before and/or after an emergency
- Create bug out plan for livestock and maintain readiness of needed equipment
- Creation of fencing or materials and plans for fencing for gardens and animal

Mechanical/Technical Skill Group

- Develop lists of needed tools and supplies to maintain, repair, and create all things mechanical. Break lists down into heavy equipment, automotive, small engine, and electronic categories. Lists should have recommended tools, spare parts, repair materials and equipment suggestions.

- Make recommendations of mechanical or technological items members should consider buying. Some SAs standardize certain equipment so parts are interchangeable.
- Keep records of warranties, replacement parts on hand, maintenance performed, and user manuals for each item in communal possession. Encourage members to do the same with their personal preps. Purchase spare parts and hardware.
- Provide training to others in the Skill Group or SG, as well as to members in general, regarding maintenance and preparation of mechanical and technological equipment such as vehicles, generators, solar powered equipment and chargers, computers etc.
- Create and maintain binder with information regarding repairs, tables and graphs needed for diagnostic and testing procedures. One binder should be for mechanical items, the other technological and includes computer, radio, communication, and phone equipment.
- Inspect/test SA equipment (except medical), perform drills, and radio checks
- Develop EMP COA (course of action) plan in conjunction with SA and SG leaders.
- Train and drill the SG and all members as needed.

Food Prep and Preservation

Unlike the **Agriculture SG** who produces food, the **Food Preparation and Preservation SG** is responsible for preparing daily meals and the preservation of any excess produce or meat for future use. Members of this group work closely with Agriculture to prepare for influxes of food for canning, dehydrating and root cellar storage. They also work with the SAL and Medical SGL to determine how much food is on hand, how much is needed and make recommendations for possible rationing. Other skills and things to have are:

- Knowledgeable about vitamin, mineral, and caloric needs for members of all ages and plan meals that are nutritious as possible.
- Know many ways to preserve food to take advantage of sales or a successful hunt prior to an emergency that interferes with the food supply. Train members so they can do the same and to build redundancy in this critical area.
- Store measuring units and both large and small food scales for use in rationing.
- Stockpile food grade buckets for storage and transportation of edibles and liquids
- Have appropriate aprons and gloves for the various tasks related to food preparation and preservation. Include "fire proof" gloves for working over fires, dish washing gloves, food handling gloves, butcher's apron, waterproof aprons, and hair nets or caps to keep hair out of food. Restaurant supply stores carry these in bulk and usually have better prices than regular grocery stores.
- Have a chart with the safe storage and serving temperature for various foods along with thermometers/gauges to monitor internal temperature of meats, measure outdoor oven temperatures and ambient temperature.
- Direct the collection of containers and materials for storing dried herbs, spices, and packing meals to be delivered to members who cannot leave their duties.
- Anticipate uses for food packaging and save accordingly. For example, tuna, chicken, and cat food come in cans that can be used to make simple cook stoves.

Morale Skills Group

Morale covers all areas maintaining mental health (except medication) and is as important to survival as food and water. If you are emotionally crippled you cannot carry out your assignments, think clearly, or support anyone else. Depression, traumatic shock, fear, insomnia, sleep disturbed by nightmares, and anger can all take their toll on an individual during and after an emergency or disaster. Helping SA members cope with stress and watching for warning signs that a member needs support is critical to SA success. It is also necessary to provide social opportunities and spiritual guidance within the group.

Regardless of age, everyone needs to have fun and relax. This can often be difficult under prolonged emergency circumstances. Even brief diversions can bring much needed stress relief. Young children, because of their age and developmental level, are not able to put aside their boredom, fear, or frustration because of a specific situation for very long. This neediness can put a strain on SA members who are trying to accomplish their assigned duties. A supervised diversion is needed to help the group function smoothly. Even adults need the stress relief that a game, music, reading, or dance can bring. The difference is that adults have a much higher tolerance for upheaval than children.

In addition to the need for diversion and recreation, everyone will at some point need the advice or listening ear of a counselor or clergy member. Individuals acting in this capacity can help SA members deal with their fear, frustrations, and help settle the disagreements that will invariably come up. Confidentiality between the "counselor" and the counseled is very important. If trust is to be developed, members must have faith that their communications are private. The only exceptions should be those that govern professionals and their clients. These are generally admissions of wrong doing that is of imminent danger to the group or to a minor. Each SA will need to determine the degree to which they wish to make exceptions. Good communication between the Morale SGL and the SAL is critical. An accurate assessment of how the group and specific individuals are doing emotionally is essential to good SA planning.

Although all members of the Alliance are encouraged to be supportive of one another, organized encouragement and recognition is an administrative function of the Morale Skills Group. The Morale Skills Group Leader or Morale SGL should formally recognize the achievement of admission requirements, completion of special training, or other contributions to the Alliance. Having a specific person track progress and provide recognition and encouragement helps new members reach their goals faster and easier. SA leadership can use feedback from Special Needs SGL to plan training, review SA regulations and otherwise improve the Alliance.

Special Care Skill Group

Almost every Survival Alliance will have some children and/or senior citizens in the membership. Both groups have special needs that require a unique set of talents and skills. At their extremes, the young and old are weaker, have more fragile immune systems and may not have the same cognitive abilities of other members. Pregnant and nursing mothers have specific requirements and limitations that must be taken into account. Some SAs will have members who have physical or cognitive disabilities. Activities and care for individuals in these categories are an important and necessary part of maintaining normal family life and group structure. Special attention must be given to temperature regulation and physical stamina, especially when outdoors or during power outages.

SA planning should include a combination of short and long-term response plans for meeting the needs of children, elders, and those with disabilities within the group. There are many good websites that offer excellent ideas for feeding, teaching and entertaining babies, toddlers and young children. Printing a selection of appropriate information and preparing supplies in advance will prove to be a blessing in an emergency. Although the old saying goes," If momma ain't happy - nobody's happy"; anyone with young children knows that it's the kids you need to keep happy. Due to their inability to understand many situations, they can be unreasonable when tired, hungry, bored, or scared. Even one screaming baby can make everyone miserable. Understanding the physical and cognitive development of children and the aging process in adults is vital to teaching, providing recreational activities, and caring for SA members in these opposing ends of life's spectrum. Coordination with the Medical SG (skill group) will ensure the best results for all.

Home nursing skills are essential to caring for the sick and injured. If professional care is not available, look for home nursing text books and online videos to learn techniques helpful to the Special Care SG. Many of these books can be found at second hand bookstores because colleges constantly change the books for courses.

CHAPTER 15

Leadership Structure

Every group needs structure and leadership. In an SA this is especially important, as the circumstances in which members come together may often be less than ideal. Leadership structure provides clear cut directions for members with problems, grievances or questions. Members must keep in mind that compliance with structure and leadership in a group that is so interdependent is essential. As nice as it sounds to give everyone a choice of what they do, it isn't practical. Rules must be made to provide order and dictate consequences for violations. Someone must enforce the rules and make the hard decisions within their stewardship. What those rules are and the consequences for breaking them are up to each SA.

If you are forming your own SA, you have the luxury of laying much of the foundation for structure and leadership. Meeting with the members of your core group to draft basic rules will give everyone a voice in the process. If you already have several individuals or families you'd like to approach, consider involving them in creating the full range of rules and structure for the Alliance. In my opinion, the founding individual and land owner of your bug-out location should have significant leadership responsibility. This is because they usually bear the greatest liability, investment of time and financial output connected to the group.

For SAs concerned about the possibility of long-term disruption of basic services and rule of law, compliance with rules and leadership requests takes on a more serious tone. If you cannot depend on law enforcement for protection, your SA will be responsible for defending itself. Decisions regarding defense, food distribution and internal problems will need to be made and members should be willing to support those choices. If there is no rule of law, tough decisions must be made. How will you handle criminals who interact with the group, defense issues, and even serious wrong doing within the group? Choose rules and leaders wisely as you will be obliged to abide by their decisions.

Although founders and bug-out location owners should have significant input within the SA, elections can be a good way to share the responsibility of leadership. Term limits for some or all positions give others the opportunity to serve or change on certain policies. Elections give a framework in which individuals can be released from their duties and other members to replace them. Each group can choose how democratic they want their SA to be. Family Alliances may function differently than primarily unrelated members of other SAs. Regardless of how you select, leaders, loyalty to these leaders must be earned and maintained by hard work, honesty and serving the best interest of the Alliance.

The legislative and judicial role can be made up of a committee of three called a **triumvirate** in ancient Rome, (see example below) or the group can vote as unlegislated situations arise. The model below works well as it provides the **SAL** (SA Leader) with two **Skill Group Leaders** with whom to confer. These three individuals can have equal authority, requiring a majority vote amongst them for a decision to be carried out. Another form of governance would be for the decisions of the SAL to be the product of consultation with the other two. All actions not covered by SA rules and Standard Operating Policies or SOPs will be decided by the SAL.

By having all **SGL** (Skill Group Leaders) report to one of the three members of the council, the leader is better able to focus on the whole group. During leadership council meetings, the assistants can provide an overview of issues in a more efficient manner than separate discussions with everyone with a grievance, needs or idea. While any member may discuss any topic with an SAL, it provides a vehicle for streamlining a potentially large amount of information and allowing some things to be delegated to each of the three members of the committee.

Each Skill Group has a designated leader or **SGL** to whom members report information, needs and problems. These leaders report to a designated **Chief**. The **Chiefs** report to the SA Commander/Leader as illustrated above. It is recommended that a SGL have no more than 15 people under their supervision. Ten is better, if that is possible. Remember, that some of these people may be in more than one group. If so, they report problems or concerns and pass information related to that Skill Group to that SGL. Concerns of a personal nature, not related to the functioning of the SG, can be shared with the Morale Officer or SA clergy member, if your group has one. Children who are too young to be assigned to an SG can be the responsibility of the **Special Care** SGL along with the adults who serve in that SG **or** their parent's primary SGL.

Survival Alliance Chain of Command and Responsibility

SG members report to Skill Group Leaders (SGLs). SGLs report to their designated Chief Officer (Defense or Medical) and the Chief SGLs report to the SA Leader or SAL. Chief SGLs or CSGLs counsel with the SAL to make decisions for the group. Your SA can give these three individuals equal authority or CSGLs, Chief Skill Group Leaders can serve as advisors to the SAL who has the final word. You can also create specific issues in your SOP manual (standard operating practices) that must be voted on by the group. Any issues not covered by the SOP will be decided by the SAL or governing council. As you can see there are lots of options.

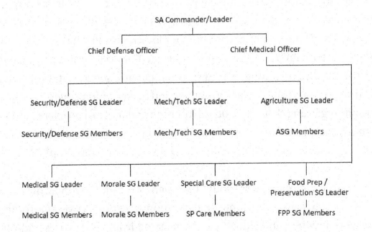

If you are organizing a large SA or combining 2 or more SAs, consider the implementation of additional Chief SGLs to whom SGLs report. These are in addition to the council of three (if you go that route). This limit the number of individuals needing to speak to the top leadership in your Alliance and streamlines the processing of information. Even if your SA is small at first, **plan for rapid expansion** when disaster strikes. This can be a temporary influx of people that you may choose to help after a natural disaster or during an episode of civil unrest. In these cases, the additional people are only temporary parts of your structure, but still require accounting for and representation. Be sure to maintain operational security as it is impossible to vet most of these people.

In some cases, you may experience a need to recruit more members to meet your needs or for a specific event. It is better to have the structure in place and functioning smoothly than working out the bugs of a new system in a time of crisis. Make copies of the form you choose or create, so they are ready for use. Many disasters result in power outages, so don't count on computer or copy service availability. In additions to administrative forms, consider creating signs indicating locations of things you feel you can handle. Signage examples include:

- **Triage**
- **Medical**
- **Sign In**
- **Volunteers**
- **Feeding Station**
- **Men / Women**
- **Keep Out**
- **No Trespassing**
- **Directional Arrows**

There are many ways to make signs. We recommend laminating a few on card stock or poster board in case rain is a factor. Panel weight wood is perfect for signs that can be nailed to a surface or made into pickets. For easier storage, do not attach the signs to pickets. Bundle the pickets, which can be bought at stores that sell lumber, along with a heavy-duty plastic bag of nails to attach the signs. Use duct tape or zip ties to attach the bag of nails to the bundle of pickets and store with the signs. When you need them, everything is ready to go. We keep two sets of signs. The first ones are those needed for the most common problems in our area. The second bundle has signs more appropriate to a long-term scenario or disaster. Most signs need directional arrows on them. You can make multiple versions of the same sign and place as needed or use permanent markers or paint to add arrows after the disaster.

Short term sign suggestions

- **DETOUR (use yellow background for better visibility)**
- **BASIC FIRST AID STATION (used to direct neighbors during clean up)**
- **DANGER (use orange for impact)**
- **KEEP OUT**
- **NO TRESPASSING (light background color)**
- **HIGH WATER (yellow background)**
- **VOLUNTEER CHECK IN**
- **HAND WASHING STATION**

Longer term sign suggestions

- **CHECK IN**
- **TRIAGE**
- **MORGUE**
- **LATRINE and OCCUPIED / OPEN and MEN/ WOMEN (if you have both)**
- **MESS HALL/DINING AREA/FOOD/ (depending upon your style and size)**
- **WARNING: TRESSPASERS WILL BE ARRESTED/DETAINED/SHOT**
- **POTABLE WATER and NON-POTABLE– DO NOT DRINK**
- **WASH HANDS BEFORE HANDLING FOOD**

These steps represent a great deal of effort, but is more than worth it. In the event of an emergency, you will be able to respond quicker and with less stress because of pre-planning. Whether you are directly affected by an emergency or are coming to the aid of others, clear leadership and organization make all the difference.

CHAPTER 16
Additional Skill Acquisition

As with food and gear, skill acquisition should be done in an orderly fashion and be supported by the group. Below is a list of specialties to illustrate the types of talents and knowledge needed for a successful group. The following examples require specialized training:

- Hunting
- Tracking
- Fishing
- Cooking
- Gardening
- Food Preservation
- Medical
- Home Health Care
- Construction – wood
- Masonry
- Metal working
- Outdoor/ camping
- Military / LEO
- Foraging
- Herbal medicine
- Communications- ham radio
- Technical/computer
- Mechanical/engineering
- Education – early childhood, primary and secondary
- Psychology & counseling
- Spiritual Guidance

Below are a few skills sets that are good to have multiple members able to perform. I have provided a breakdown of the skill heading to help illustrate the many things that one word can imply. This can be helpful when choosing someone to train for a specific skill. Seeing the components or characteristics that indicate aptitude can focus your selection process.

Hunting

- Knowledge of the behavior, signs, and habitats of various game
- Good marksmanship skills specific to rifle, shotgun, and/or bow

- Ability to field dress game and transport the animal
- Butcher skills to break carcass down into various cuts
- Patience and conservation awareness
- Camouflage and scent reduction skills
- Ability to make or perform game calls

Tracking /Scouting

- Ability to read the signs of animal and human movement
- Orienteering skills
- Knowledge of weather lore and natural indicators
- Rappelling and climbing experience
- Various forms of nonverbal communication such as Morse code mirror flash
- Signal flag or hand signals knowledge

Fishing

- Knowledge of fish habits, habitat preferences, and appropriate bait/lure
- Ability to maintain and repair fishing equipment
- Good knot tying skills for lines and nets
- Cleaning fish, crustaceans, and mollusks
- Ability to make lures and flies

Off-grid Cooking

- Fire starting skills – under various conditions for different styles of cooking
- Skilled in use of various types of stoves, ovens, grills & cast iron
- Can care for and repair specialized cookware and ovens
- Can improvise various types of stoves, ovens and smokers

Gardening

- Knowledge of plants which grow in the area.
- Knowledgeable about edible and poisonous plants
- Ability to use organic methods for fertilization and pest control.
- Working knowledge of manual methods of tilling, planting, and harvesting food
- Understand the concept of companion planting to maximize harvest
- Skill with the farming tools common to pioneer era farmers

Medical

Access to medical care in any emergency is very important. As you look for people in this category, remember that there are many levels and types of medical skill. Encourage members of your family and Survival Alliance to learn medical skills whenever they can.

Many communities offer Red Cross Basic and Advanced First Aid, CPR, and similar classes at reasonable prices. Local vo-techs offer reasonably priced courses that offer certification upon completion for EMT and paramedic as well as nursing courses such as CNA, CMA and individual home nursing skills. Whether you intend to use these skills professionally or not, they are valuable in your daily life and in an emergency. Some certifications lapse if not used in a job setting within a certain amount of time. Look for ways to keep your certification from lapsing. If it does, you must usually take the whole course again. If you find yourself needing these skills to provide for your family, current certification would be a great help.

In addition to Western allopathic medicine, consider developing alternative medicine skills as well. Many remedies are based on plants that can be grown in your garden and preserved for future use. Knowing what plants can be used to treat what ailments is also a very valuable skill. There are many books and websites devoted to herbal medicine. There are campus classes and even online courses that offer training and certification. Individual classes are also available from many places. Online tutorials are also available free of charge on various sites. Be sure to check the information from individuals with professional sources to be sure it is safe.

In addition to herbal medicine be sure to investigate massage therapy, acupressure, and similar types of treatments. These can ease pain and help heal injuries as well as prevent many ailments. In addition to formal schooling, there are great tutorials for these techniques as well. They are often easy and inexpensive to learn. These skills are valuable any time, but especially when muscles ache or injuries interfere with daily duties and responsibilities.

Remember traditional and modern approaches to healthcare and fill with both for maximum options. If you cannot find people who are already trained, consider pooling group resources to help an existing member get trained. In addition to subsidizing the cost of classes, members can be supportive by helping with child care and other domestic responsibilities. If illness or injury strikes within the alliance, medical skills and supplies will be priceless, so make this a top priority.

CHAPTER 17

Training and Practice

Every Survival Alliance will consist of individuals of varying skill and fitness level. Training and practice are needed to help individual members grow into an effective team. This can be instruction presented by knowledgeable members or provided by outside professionals. Whether through individual or group instruction, it is essential that members gain basic required skills and then move on to more advanced topics.

Our family has taken the **CERT or Citizens Emergency Response Team** training, several times over a period of four years from the city of Newcastle in central Oklahoma. We are grateful to the Emergency Management, Fire and Storm Shelter management for this resource. Not all cities offer this program. We highly recommend finding a town that operates a CERT or offers CERT training. Newcastle was a forty-five-minute drive for us, but well worth it.

If you can't find CERT training within reasonable driving distance, look online. This training is available on line and many chapters produce educational videos. CERT falls under the jurisdiction of Homeland Security and provides excellent training that helps citizens be better prepared to reduce and respond to hazards in their lives. Individuals that want to can volunteer in their communities to serve their neighbors. We trained and volunteered with a neighboring town because our town did not have a CERT. Our family helped with things from directing traffic during yearly vaccination clinics and local festivals to manning the city tornado shelter before serious weather events and tornado clean up. This training and service was a wonderful bonding experience and gave my boys skills to take with them as they left home. I highly encourage CERT training, whether you are preparing to care for your family or community.

Mental Planning Exercises

It has been said that focused mental practice of a physical skill can often be as effective as actually performing the action. This is especially true of self-defense and danger avoidance. Never underestimate the value of advanced planning. Making decisions about how you would react to a given situation and mentally rehearsing that scenario is a very effective tool. My father used to tell me, "See the scenario unfolding in your mind's eye in detail. See yourself taking the action you have decided is appropriate." Deciding what you should do in various situations well in advance reduces fear in the moment and decreases reaction time. Vivid mental rehearsal also increases your confidence in your ability to carry out the appropriate response. The key is to walk through each scenario in detail. See yourself responding appropriately and being successful. Don't be afraid to explore variations of the same situation. Consider scenarios in which the chosen response is not successful and work from there to choose an alternate response. Combining mental rehearsal with practicing with a partner will provide the best results.

Some scenarios regarding personal safety can be frightening to even contemplate. Despite this, realistic visualization of foreseeable dangers can save your life or the life of someone you love. Some of the most common personal safety threats are:

- Robbery/mugging
- Abduction
- Sexual assault
- Mob violence (motivated by racial, ethnic, religious, economic or gender factors)

Each of these dangers could unfold in a multitude of ways. Writing scenario cards provide a way to cover them individually and provides an opportunity to train with your SA members. Provide details like time of day, location, lighting, environment such as big city sidewalks at noon or a field of tall grass not far from a grove of trees at dusk. Indicate the number of friendlies and hostiles. These factors greatly influence the decision process and are very important.

In addition to personal safety threats, consider the other dangers one could face in an emergency or post disaster scenario. These are excellent problem-solving exercises and can include:

- Getting from work to home or school to home after a disaster.
- Getting to a bug out retreat in a vehicle
- Getting to a bug out retreat on foot.
- Finding water in an urban/rural setting
- Navigating a crowd outside a Red Cross station
- Dealing with gridlock traffic during an evacuation
- Encountering a demonstration while leaving work
- Dealing with a flat tire at night in a rough part of the city.

Another preparedness measure for your SA is what Scouts call a **shakedown**. This is a planned verification of required gear that often includes an opportunity to use it. These are usually done in preparation for high adventure trips to insure participants have the required gear and know how to use it. This makes the high adventure safer and more fun. If there is a problem with gear, it is better to have it pop up in a local campground instead of on a mountain side or deep in the woods on a fifty-mile hike.

Read any good books lately?

Despite the value of hands on instruction and online tutorial videos, the most common form of learning is reading a book. A distinct advantage of books is the ability to review the information, without power, as often as you want. Once read, they can be loaned to others or referenced for obscure information as needed. While some topics are subject to frequent change, the core topics of preparedness are fairly consistent. As a result of the fixed nature of topics, such as first aid, camping skills, orienteering, bush craft etc., bargains can be found at second hand book stores. Taking advantage of this savings frees up money for other purchases. Garage sales are another source of instructional and reference books. Public and school libraries often hold sales of donated or older books as fund raisers. These books are even more affordable than second hand stores. Since some institutions have annual sales, ask when it's held. Put the date on the group's calendar and encourage members to buy helpful titles.

Military manuals are great sources of information on first aid, security, and defense. Many are available at public libraries, and for sale in book stores, online vendors, and as e-books. If you choose e-books, consider printing the most important information for use if no power is available or the device it is stored on is destroyed. We purchased an extra Kindle and downloaded important books and information to it. It is stored in a mini Faraday cage. Just in case something happens to it, we have put condensed versions of the most critical information in a binder for easy transport.

In addition to e-books, start a lending library for your group. Many of us have books we no longer need. Once a skill has graduated to intermediate or advanced level, consider donating beginner books to the SA. These books can help others learn without the expense of purchasing them.

Physical Fitness

It is fairly safe to say that most of us could be in better shape. Even if a person is not over weight, they may be out of shape. Building stamina for physical activity and tolerance for heat and cold make weathering most emergencies easier. In addition to attaining a healthy weight and increasing general stamina, conditioning muscles that we don't use much is important. If you are not accustomed to walking or hiking, a long-distance trek could be miserable and take much longer than necessary. The following activities use muscles the average person will need to strengthen:

- Carrying a filled backpack – 20-30 lbs.
- Rowing a boat or canoe, climbing or rappelling
- Standing for extended periods of time
- Outdoor chores like chopping wood or digging holes
- Repeatedly lifting heavy items like wood, sand bags or hay bales
- Hiking, running and walking especially on uneven surfaces
- Stooping to weed, rake, hoe or pick produce from your garden

It is wise to visit with your doctor before beginning any fitness regimen. I am not saying that for liability purposes, but because it can be very helpful. Discuss your desire to get in shape with someone who knows your medical conditions and any limitations you may have. Your doctor may give you advice on activities that you should avoid based on your specific condition. If you have limitations due to previous injuries, surgery, or other medical conditions, consider using the services of a physical therapist or certified physical trainer. They can help tailor a program to your needs that will allow you to build strength and stamina safely. If you do not have any serious health issues, a good personal trainer can help you select exercises that target muscle groups you need to build. They can recommend the number of repetitions and proper form required to get the results you are looking for. Once you have the basics down, you can work out on your own. Periodic consultations can help you be sure you are doing the exercises correctly and allow you to adjust your work out as you progress.

Group exercise and work projects are great ways to team build while getting healthy. The more members get outside and do physical activities, the easier it is to do. Over time, many people can increase their tolerance for hot and cold weather. This provides an opportunity to learn how to dress appropriately and to identify symptoms of various forms of exposure. As parents or leaders of a skill group or an entire alliance, such activities help identify those who are truly unable to tolerate extremes of temperatures or much physical exertion. This information is valuable when making job assignments within the group. Remember to be positive and supportive of healthy life style changes of all SA members. This encouragement can be the difference between discouragement and giving up and sticking to a program.

CHAPTER 18

Preparing Children and Teens

While it is important that adults be prepared to deal with the unexpected, don't forget the kids. They need to be prepared as well. The same reasons that adults should use mental preparation exercises also apply to young people. Mental preparation is the most important part of emergency preparedness. If you haven't considered the emergency situations you should prepare for, you can't buy the appropriate supplies. If you have supplies but don't know how to use them, you aren't prepared. On the other hand, if you have knowledge but no supplies available during an emergency occurs, you can still react appropriately and often get what you need.

Remember that children are usually much more capable of learning new things than we think they are. If given age appropriate information and support during the learning process, kids can learn all kinds of things. The key to teaching children is to make it fun. After almost 25 years of volunteering with Boy Scouts of America I believe in the slogan "Scouting is fun with a purpose." Leaders should remember that. If we want to help the young people in our lives become well rounded and prepared, we need to remember to create learning opportunities that are fun and challenging. It is also important to take advantage of teachable moments. These moments happen all the time and can even be created. These lessons often have greater impact because they spring from something real and relevant in our lives. You can make wonderful memories and bond while teaching a life lesson or skill.

With the rise in active shooter incidents and terrorism, it's smart to talk about how your children should respond in these scenarios. Learn what protocols are in place in their schools and any other place they spend time regularly, such as church or sporting practice and games. If they are not adequate, in your opinion, work to bring about change. You can speak to the principal, superintendent, police department, and/or city emergency manager to gather information about how threats are handled. Be careful how you phrase your questions so as not to arouse suspicion. Some homegrown terrorists might ask similar questions to prepare an attack. Respect the fact that they may not be able to give the details you'd like. It is fair to expect information about:

- Frequency of fire and tornado drills
- Do teachers have any special training?
- Are any administrators or teachers armed? Is there on campus security?
- Does the school have tornado shelters and where are they located?
- Lock down procedure – What students are expected to do during lock downs?
- Has city emergency management and police prepared for active shooter, bomb threat, and/or abduction scenarios? Do they offer response training to teachers and students?

Every parent must make their own decisions about how they want their children to respond to dangerous situations. These decisions should be based on factors such as:

- Age and maturity of the child
- Special skills or training
- Neighborhood crime rates
- Circumstances such as messy divorces or custody cases

My husband and I talked with each of our children about specific scenarios and gave customized advice and instructions. Our sons have had extensive Scout, leadership, and first responder training so they were well equipped to handle themselves. We discussed the responsibility to stay safe and then help others. Taking control of situations in which people are confused, scared, and need direction to stay safe is an important role. We discussed the fact that there are also times when there is nothing you can do. We talked about their school emergency protocols and made suggestions of what they could do to be smarter or safer in some cases. We emphasized that each scenario is different and requires some real-time decision making. We encourage all parents to have age appropriate discussions with their children that reflect their values, training and abilities.

Our oldest son and a fellow Scout used their first aid training to assist a friend in choir who had a seizure during a competition. The adults around them either had no idea what to do or were trying to implement wives-tales as first aid. The boys explained the proper seizure response and helped place the student in the recovery position afterwards until the ambulance arrived. Both teens were glad they knew what to do.

Our second son was awarded the Boy Scout Award for Meritorious Action for the first aid he rendered when a fellow student was stabbed in his yard near the school. Our son was friends with the young man and was at his home visiting his younger brother. All the boys belonged to the same Boy Scout troop and church. Our son attended to his injured friend and instructed neighbors to call EMS, the police, and bring needed supplies. He told me later that night that he was worried the adults would not listen to him. When he asked a man to bring something, the man asked if he was a Boy Scout. My son told him he was, and the man told the group to do what he said. My son told me that he was scared, but was surprised at how his training popped to the front of his brain when he needed it. He also confided that when he had a moment to himself a few hours later, he threw up. We were so proud and grateful to all the people that contributed to our sons' knowledge and other youth each year through various scouting organizations. Because of this instruction, young people do similar things under all kinds of conditions every year. They are capable of tremendous courage, clarity, and ingenuity. Empower and educate them to be a force for good in the world. Consider enrolling your children in a scouting program or Red Cross training for youth or sharing your time and talent as a leader or instructor.

In addition to training, giving responsibilities to youth can help them mature and become more confident. Assigning duties is an important method for teaching responsibility. To help children gain work ethics, help them learn the connection between their choices and what follows. Protecting them from the consequences of their decisions is a disservice that can stunt maturity. Your objective should be to help your children and the youth you work with, to become thinking, dependable, members of society and your Survival Alliance. I love the saying, "A stumble prevents a fall.", which encourages us to let them fail sometimes. **Lessons learned as children are rarely as costly as those postponed until adulthood.** Losing computer privileges for a day for being late for school, due to a misplaced backpack, is better than losing your job because you failed to learn organization or punctuality.

Traits like obedience, dependability, trustworthiness, integrity, and work ethic are not just important to the development of a good citizen, who is right with his Maker. These traits may save their life or the lives of others in a crisis. For these reasons, it is the responsibility of parents, extended family and the Alliance to help youth members fulfill their potential. Proverbs 22:6 offers this wisdom, "Train up a child in the way he should go: and when he is old he will not depart from it."

There are a lot of things you can do in your everyday life to impart these character traits. One of the best places to start is teaching cause and effect; the concept of consequences. Even toddlers are capable of learning simple examples. They quickly learn that if they press a specific point on a toy, that it speaks or plays music. They learn when they hit or throw things, they are stopped and told not to. Pointing out and discussing expected outcomes builds **critical thinking skills**. Playing cause and effect games can program young minds to anticipate outcomes to action. As they grow, this will enable them to apply reason to new situations. In time, this will lead to the ability to make good choices in personal safety and emergency situations. Initial "training" should be part of the activities of daily living and be **fun**. Children learn best through fun, repetitious activities. Young children should be provided opportunities to learn self-control, discipline, responsibility, and service. These traits will make them better able to handle stressful situations. They will be **flexible** when things are different than usual. They will be better able to **adapt** to emergency situations if they have taught to think about the consequences of actions. What a wonderful gift to give a young person and the world. Don't be discouraged. Just set smart family and SA rules and mentor the children in your life to be ready for the challenges ahead. The resulting skills will be well worth it. Here are some mentoring tips:

- Personal responsibility can be taught by giving age appropriate responsibility for putting away the things they own or use.
- **Accountability and responsibility** can be taught by assigning chores and attaching positive re-enforcement for compliance. Withholding of privileges should be used for failure to do assignments. Be sure the task is within the ability of the child.
- Skills can be taught by making activities such as gardening, cooking, or caring for animals a family affair. Even watching has value and can lead to a body of knowledge. Again, give **age appropriate opportunities** to all children in the family or group. Children can also be paired with an older sibling or parent for mentoring.
- Child size equipment, whether for play or helping, is a great way to involve kids. Pint sized shovels, spades, rakes, and brooms make it easier and safer for kids to be involved.
- Enrolling children in organizations such as scouting groups, FFA and FHA or signing them up for private instruction is a great way to help them learn skills you may not have. Research resources in your area and involve the child in the choice of activity. It is important to expect them to finish the contract, season, event or year associated with the activity. This will help instill **commitment and perseverance.**

CHAPTER 19

Used and Homemade Gear and Supplies

Up-cycled and Recycled Prep Gear

Thrift stores, garage sales, and personal ads are great places to get used preparedness gear.* Most of the time, the items are being sold because the owner rarely, if ever used them. We've all purchased something that was bought under the influence of an infomercial or the rave review of a friend and ended up never using it. Whether the trend passed or they didn't have time for it, you can scoop it up at a big savings. My favorite steals were a crate of brand new Lodge cast ironware for $25 and 8 life vests in assorted sizes for $20. Look for signs that gear has been exposed to heat or sunlight for prolonged periods of time. This can cause fibers and plastics to weaken or become brittle.

Remember to look for items that can be used to produce preps too. People often donate craft and hobby supplies. Below is a list my favorite things to look for at garage sales, thrift stores and in classifieds.

- **Backpacks, duffle bags, and luggage** can be expensive and preppers need so many to store and transport supplies. Look for high quality pack with a lot of pockets to help you stay organized. 72 hour packs for each member of the family can be very affordable using secondhand packs. Carry on size luggage with wheels and a collapsible handle are great for extra water or other heavy items. This type of pack is most commonly used for the most common emergencies, which are brief in nature and only effect small geographic areas. In these instances, families often evacuate to a friend or extended family members' house or a Red Cross shelter. Being able to pull your pack instead of carrying it is perfect for this limited use situation. For larger, more extensive packs, look for heavy duty back packs and duffle bags.

- You can even find military issued or mil spec versions if you keep an eye out. Inspect all items carefully. Many items are donated because of zippers that catch or are missing hardware. Some items have small tears or holes. If the piece is a high-quality piece that you need, consider the possibility of repairing it. Many fabric and upholstery shops have a wide selection of buttons, snaps, latches, webbing and clasps with tools to attach them. Most of these repairs are simple and take very little time. If a heavy duty sewing machine is required, shoe repair and saddle shops can often make the repair for a modest fee.

- **Candles**, new or used, can be found everywhere. The cheapest per pound are often the big, decorative ones. You are after the wax so the outward appearance of the candle does not matter. Scented or unscented candles are fine. Just remember that strongly scented candles should not be used if detection is a concern. If the breeze carries the scent of Pumpkin Spice or Hot Apple Pie, you may wind up with uninvited guests. Although not dangerous, strongly scented candle wax may not make the best tuna can burner as perfume or floral scents can clash with food having an unappetizing effect. On the other hand, if you're hungry I doubt that it will stop anyone. Scented wax can be used for heat and light sources. Remember to use a designated pot to melt wax for any purpose. Such a pot can be found at a garage sale or thrift store for next to nothing. Candles can be melted to make many different fire starters. My favorites are dipped pine cones, cardboard egg carton starters, and tuna can burners. If the candle is large, save the wick for reuse. You can also buy wicks and pour new candles.

- Pots, pans and other cookware are also readily available for pennies on the dollar. Look for heavy duty pots, pans and cookie sheets which will stand up to use. Avoid used Teflon coated pans as they are usually scratched leading to human consumption of flaking bits. Instead look for cast iron, heavy stainless and large stock and water bath canning pots.
- **Pressure cookers** make short work of big jobs like roasts and large amounts of root veggies like potatoes, carrots, and parsnips. Dry beans in a pressure cooker cook in minutes instead of hours and use much less water. Replacement gaskets and other lid parts can be found online. Just look for the manufacturer and the model number or name. I buy my replacement parts off Amazon. Manufacturer's instructions for use can often be found online as well.
- **Food dehydrators** are easy to find and instructions for specific models can be found at most manufacturers websites.
- **Can openers** can be found in the utensil section of most thrift stores and at many garage sales. I have a five-gallon bucket full of them. In the event of a disaster, non-perishable goods are distributed, but I have never seen can openers passed out. If people must evacuate, they are unlikely to think of can openers. If canned food is passed out or scavenged, can openers will be a necessity. They make a good item to share as service or for bartering. Other utensils to look for are long handled grilling tools, cast iron lifting hooks, cooling racks (for bread in bulk) and knives. For those who are preparing for long term scenarios, a large selection of knives for butchering and processing game and livestock is critical. Fillet knives, scalers, and bread knives are also important. Sharpen and store these separate from your daily use utensils for portability. Remember to purchase a sharpening stone and oil and learn how to use them.
- Secondhand bookstores are wonderful sources of books with all kinds of information. There are cook books, camping guides, medical reference books, repair manuals, plant identification and foraging guides and more at a fraction of their original cost. Keep in mind that there is no electricity in many emergency scenarios. Hard copy information is important when internet or computer files are not available.
- **Camping gear** such as tents, propane stoves, large water dispensers, and ice chests are often sold or donated when they are no longer needed or wanted. I have purchased many such items when the owner underestimated the rigors of hiking, camping or rafting. One gentleman sold me his brand-new cast ironware because his wife refused to cook outdoors because of "creepy crawlies". As with all purchases, inspect the items carefully. Are all the pieces there? If not, how likely and expensive is replacement? Pull out that smart phone and search on the spot to avoid wasting money. If you find a cheap second-hand version of an item you already have, consider buying it for **spare parts**. Sometimes broken or damaged items are free for the taking. Stripping it of knobs, gaskets, hardware or grills is a great way to have replacements for essential gear. Use heavy duty freezer bags for parts. I put small pieces in snack size zipper bags and label where they go on what piece of equipment. Put the small bags in a larger, labeled freezer bag.
- **Winter wear** is easy to find, as many people don't want to store bulky clothing until next winter and children outgrow things so fast. Women's items are more common as many *fashionistas* won't wear last seasons' style the following year. For more information on clothing, see Appendix 2 – **Clothing Checklist**.

(Never buy used carabiners unless you really trust the seller. Dropping these can cause metal fatigue over time leading to failure. Also, be wary of climbing ropes. If not cared for properly they can wear in places you can't see and drastically shorten their life or cause failure.)

Not all gear or supply items are available or safe secondhand. Be sure to take advantage of what is. You can save a ton of money that can be used for the things you need to buy new or for high end splurges.

Don't forget that lots of preps can be made by recycling things you usually throw away. Many sites have clever ideas for turning trash into treasure. Check out **repurposing ideas** on **Pinterest** and similar sites. Some of my favorites are:

- Tuna/chicken can burners
- Dryer lint and pine cone fire starters
- Cravats, slings and bandages made from old sheets
- Using sterilized soda and juice bottles to store dry foods like beans or rice

If you find a clever idea but don't use the product needed to make it, ask friends and family to save the item for you. People with cats often feed wet food or tuna and can save the **cans** for your buddy burner project. If you want to store some of your dry staples for short term use, ask friends or church members to save large **plastic juice jugs** for you. You don't have to be specific about why. I usually just say it's for a craft project I saw online. School cafeterias, senior living centers and large day cares will often save empty **#10 cans** for you. If you want the cans for rocket stoves or similar projects, ask for cans that held vegetables. These require little effort to clean out compared to pudding, cream soups or sticky fruits like peaches and pears. To make it simple for them and harder to say no, don't ask for the cans to be washed out and pick them up that day. This is also true of **5 gallon buckets**. The best contents are frosting or syrups. These ingredients smell good and are more pleasant to clean out. Pungent ingredients such as soy sauce, pickles, or dairy products can sink into the plastic and taint the food you store inside with an unappealing odor or flavor. Always express your gratitude. You may want them to do this for you or your group another time. Take 5 gallon buckets to the **car wash** and spray them out with the high-pressure hose. This keeps most of the residue out of your tub and pipes. Finish up at home with dish soap, brush and hot water.

My last tips for used gear is placing a **want ad** in local papers and online forums like Craig's List. Sometimes people don't think about selling items they don't use. They don't have enough for a yard sale or they don't want to bother with one. They may have even forgotten about an item they haven't used in a long time. Your request can draw their attention to it. Also share what you are looking for on your community center and church bulletin board or website. The seller gets a little extra cash and you get a great deal on something you need. Another way of doing this is **asking** about items you don't see at a garage sale. I once asked about mason jars at an estate sale. The granddaughter went in the garage and came back to tell me she had about 200 in boxes. She asked $20 for all of them just to get rid of them. When I asked her why she hadn't put them out, she explained she didn't think that anyone canned anymore. The moral of the story is that you never know unless you ask. The worst that can happen is you get told no. Happy hunting!

CHAPTER 20

Sheltering in Place

When many think of prepping, they think of bugging out to a remote location. The truth is, it is much more likely that sheltering in place will be your best move. It is as important to know how to shelter in place safely and effectively, as it is to gain roughing it skills and choosing a retreat position.

The most common emergencies are ones that require individuals and families to stay where they are and wait until danger has passed. Common reasons to shelter in place are:

- Severe thunder storms
- Tornado warning
- Ice or snow storm
- Wide spread power outage

Less common, but equally important are:

- Civil unrest
- Prisoner escape
- Criminal / police chase
- Looting after natural disaster
- Quarantine due to illness (ordered or self-imposed)

We live in a mobile, buy on demand culture. If you are hungry, you hop in the car and go get take-out food or visit your favorite restaurant. No prep time or dishes. Sounds like a winner, right? On second glance, we notice that this has a down side. Folks who eat out all the time have very little food in the refrigerator and cupboards. They spend much more per meal and rarely eat as healthy as they would if they cooked at home. I am not suggesting that eating out is all bad and that no one ever should. I am suggesting that all this eating in the car on the way home or to Jr.'s soccer practice can have a negative impact on our preparedness. Like most things in life, moderation is the key.

Look through your cupboards, refrigerators, and closets. Make a list of things you would need if you had to stay in your home for a day or two. How would you fair if you needed to stay in for three or four days? Think about how much toilet paper you have right now. How long until you would run out? Perishables such as milk, eggs, and bread, along with hygiene items should top the list of things to keep stocked during seasons of severe weather. Identify the things you need for your diet and lifestyle and begin building a back-stock. Then, should you need to shelter in place, you are set.

In addition to food, hygiene, and medical supplies, it is important to store things you will need to secure your home in a few common scenarios. These items will help you cope with the specific reason you are sheltering in place. Also include supplies needed to clean up and make repairs after severe weather. This will save you time and stress in the wake of damaging storms. While others are navigating debris littered roads and standing in line for the same items everyone else needs, you will be sitting pretty. Besides, streets are often blocked by downed trees and debris making getting to the store difficult or impossible. Having commonly needed supplies provides peace of mind and convenience.

Getting Ready for Storms

The first items that people run out and buy, when a storm or other disruptive event is expected, are perishables such as bread, milk, and eggs. These items are those foods we purchase often due to short shelf life. Rounding out the list of most common purchases are bottled water, soda, flashlights and batteries. Long lines at the mega-marts are common as people wait until the last minute to get the things they need. Consider keeping a good quality powdered milk, rotating frozen loaves of bread through the freezer, and keeping other items like eggs, soda, coffee, toilet paper, and tissues stocked during storm season. This will keep you from needing to stand in line for these items. Additionally, road conditions or personal safety may not be optimal. Staying home reduces unnecessary risk taking. Create a few kits designed to meet challenges the of specific situations common to your area is easy. Winter storm, hurricane, tornado, summer power outage and personal safety themes are examples of this type of kit. These kits can become a group requirement and could require training on their use.

My personal favorite kit is the what we call the **Storm Box**. This one has gotten the most mileage at our house. The contents are helpful during spring and summer thunder storms as well as winter storms. Use the list below as a guide to help you create your own.

The Storm Box/Kit

Contents are divided into three main categories: HEAT, LIGHT, and FOOD. I bought a three-drawer plastic organizer and labeled the drawers accordingly. Separate plastic tubs could also be used. If you have a large family, this is a good choice.

For the **HEAT** drawer, I stocked supplies for lighting fires for warmth, cooking, and protection. They include:

- Matches
- Lighter – stick type
- Cans of Sterno
- Fire starters (wax dipped cotton pads or dryer lint)
- Votive candles / tea lights and holders
- Instructions for set up, trouble shooting, and use of generator.

For the **LIGHT** drawer, I stocked it with items related to being able to see in the dark and indicate hazards. These include:

- Roll of reflective tape to mark cords and rope
- Flashlights – small individual size - inside
- Flashlights – large heavy duty – outside
- LED lantern for hands-free task lighting
- Glow sticks / cylume sticks
- Extra batteries for flash lights
- Hand crank charging lantern
- Flash lights for everyone in the family
- Small solar powered chargers

The last major category is **FOOD**. Having the means to heat water and cook food will be paramount. It's amazing how far a cup of hot chocolate goes towards warming you up or comforting a child's fears. Today there are so many great tasting products that only require boiling water to make. Keep foods simple and easy to prepare and include beverages that you can drink warm in cold weather. Examples are:

- Paper plates, cups and disposable cutlery
- Napkins, paper towels and wet wipes
- Dehydrated soup mixes
- Canned food easily heated
- Hot chocolate or cider
- Marshmallows for roasting
- Camp coffee pot for bowling water
- Metal camp cups with handles
- Small counter top stove (uses Sterno or votive candle)

Here is how we handle severe storms
Step 1. Stock Up

Once a significant weather event is forecasted, we top off the perishables we are low on. Since I have been lucky enough to stay home with my children instead of working outside the home, my favorite time to do this time of shopping is the middle of the night. Mega Marts are open and restock during the early morning hours. This means fewer people to deal with and freshly stocked shelves. If you wait until the day before or of the forecasted storm, you risk not getting certain items or the quantity you want due to the crowds of last minute shoppers. You will not be the only one trying to shop on the way to or from work. If forecasters are wrong and the storm is early, you may not get what you need at all.

Step 2. Straighten Up

On the day before the storm is forecasted, we catch up on any dirty laundry and dishes. The floors are swept and rugs vacuumed and the house generally tidied up. This leaves things caught up in case we lose power. A sink full of dishes or laundry room full of dirty clothes can get stinky fast, especially in warm weather. Straightening up clears clutter from the floors making it safer to move around with just a flashlight. It also makes counters and table tops safer for candles and lanterns with open flames. Don't forget to clean out the fire place as well to make plenty of room for new ash. Clear the area in front of fireplace to reduce fire hazard.

The day of the storm we switch to disposable plates and cups to reduce dishes to wash. This frees up more time for other preparations such as tending to the animals and property. If you have a garage or carport, be sure the space is clear for vehicles. Due to various projects and adult kids storing things at our house, our garage space isn't always clear enough to pull the car in. During storm season, these items and projects must be kept to a minimum and able to be moved at a moments' notice. This enables us to prevent damage to our vehicles.

Step 3. Power Up

The day before the storm, we fill both vehicles with gas. We also fill one or two 5- gallon gas cans if needed for possible generator use. We rotate the gas through our vehicles to be sure it stays fresh. We also charge our power bricks and personal devices such as cell phones, tablets and laptops. We made sure everyone downloaded a local weather app on our phones to allow for updates even if there is no electricity or we are in the storm shelter. We keep the weather radio, flash lights and rechargeable batteries ready to go.

Step 4. Rest Up

If the storm is expected in the evening, consider eating a little earlier than usual. This way dinner is over and cleaned up if the storm arrives earlier than forecasted. Otherwise, you run the risk of losing power and not eating the nice meal you planned. Another thing to get out of the way early is bathing. This way you are ready for bed and work the next day. Also, bathing during severe weather can be dangerous. If the power goes out, you are wet and in the dark trying to get out and dressed. If you rely on a well pump for water and don't have an automatic generator to kick in, you could end up with soapy hair and no water.

Many storms hit during the middle of the night making it hard to sleep. Consider having at least one adult go to bed early or take a nap during the day. This way they will be fresh during the night. It is important for someone to be alert in areas that have blizzards or tornados. Some find it hard to sleep due to noise and want to stay abreast of weather details, while others sleep right through it. Napping or going to bed early also helps you get up for school or work if your sleep is interrupted later due to the storm. Every household should find a solution that works for them.

Step 5. Listen Up

Just prior to and during a storm, we keep a local channel on so that weather updates stream across the bottom and our familiar forecasters interrupt programming with breaking information. Not everyone is good with directions (me) and many are new to the area. This can make using weather information more difficult. One of the best things I ever did for my family was to copy a simplified map of the area and labeled and shaded the counties. I then taped it inside a pantry door that all my children were tall enough to see. Should they find themselves home alone, they could look to see where the county mentioned in the weather advisory was and know if they had anything to be concerned about. You can also include information on the general movement patterns of storms common to your area. While these are generalizations, they can be helpful to planning. An example from our neck of the woods is tornado behavior. Tornados **generally** move from the west or southwest to the east or northeast. We have used this generalization to help us decide if tornado producing clouds have passed before going to bed. If there are still lines of dangerous showers that could spawn tornados that would move our way, at least one adult stays up. The same protocol applies to snow storms and blizzard. Winter storms **generally** come out of the west or northwest and tend to move east or south east. We watch these closely because of livestock. Animals require special preparation for winter storms and monitoring throughout. This monitoring allows you to catch problems as soon as they pop up, resulting in reduced hardship or even death.

We keep a weather radio, programmed for our area, on at night while we sleep during storm season or when bad weather is expected. This is very reassuring to children, as they know their parents won't miss important weather information. Living in tornado country, we need every minute of advanced warning we can get. Weather radios can be programmed to turn themselves on when weather warnings are issued. You can program the counties you wish to receive alerts from. If you are having trouble programming yours, your local fire department can assist you.

Step 6. Size Up

After the storm has passed we perform a **size up**. This term refers to the assessment of your surroundings to determine if it is safe to proceed with clean up or welfare checks. Remember that winds, rain, and various forms of precipitation can damage power lines, weaken or break tree limbs or entire trees, and cause surfaces to be slick. Before stepping outside, stand in the doorway and look above, to the sides, and on the ground. Look for loosened or hanging things that may fall and for things that pose tripping hazards. Repeat this process as you move throughout your yard and move about your property. Check on pets and livestock to be sure they are still safe and secure. Storms can damage pens and stalls leading to injury, exposure, or animals running loose. If your home or outbuildings have heavy roof or wall damage, proceed with caution. Rafter and load bearing beam damage may be severe enough to cause collapse. Evacuate if you are concerned and get a professional assessment before reentering.

Step 7. Clean Up

Once the storm has passed, another type of storm kit becomes important. The **Outdoor Storm Gear Kit** contains all the seldom used, but very important, specialized clothing and gear needed to go out in bad weather. Since we have multiple adults able to assist, we stored our kit gear in a heavy-duty plastic foot locker. These are light weight, water-proof, and many come with sturdy latches with the option to attach a lock. If you are helping with recovery and clean up at another location, you can put the foot locker in the back of a truck or on a trailer and not worry about it.

Sometimes during winter storms and after thunderstorms, we dress for the weather, grab tactical quality flashlights (extremely bright and waterproof) and go out to inspect the home and property. If it's night, the storm was not severe, and you do not have any outdoor animals, consider staying inside until morning. The only exception might be to check on exposed vehicles. If there is hail damage to the windows, you can prevent further water damage by using tarps or plastic sheeting to cover the broken windows. This should be purchased in advance from the paint supply section of hardware and superstores. Opening a door and shutting it on one end of the plastic then stretching it across to another door and doing the same on the other end, can secure the plastic even in windy conditions. Tape is not likely to stick as everything will be wet. Measuring your car windshield and rear glass and adding the wrap around through the nearest door length allows you to cut the plastic in advance. This way you won't have to do it in the rain and it can be applied quickly. Fold each piece, label it (front, back or sides), and store in a gallon size zipper bag **under the seat** of each car. By storing the plastic in the car, you will have it regardless of where you are. Watch out for broken glass which may be inside your vehicle. Wear work gloves and use a whisk broom to clear seats before entering. These items are good items to have in your auto kit as they are helpful when cleaning other types of messes.

Similar measures can be taken to prepare for **broken house windows**. Measuring and pre-cutting plastic for windows can make this a quick fix. Use a permanent marker to label the sheets and store them in a large plastic zipper bag with the name of the room on it. These sheets can also be used to decrease **airborne contaminants** from entering your home. You can attach the plastic using a staple gun directly or add pre-cut cardboard or thin wood trim to prevent tearing if the patch needs to last an extended period of time. If the windows are being sealed due to concerns about airborne contaminants, use duct tape inside the home. This reduces damage to the seal from weather and allows you to apply it without additional risk of exposure. Inspect the seal on windows periodically to be sure the tape is not peeling away from the trim or wall.

High quality plastic sheeting is sold by the roll and is cheaper than folded sheets. It comes in black and clear. Each have their advantages. Clear plastic allows light in and is helpful during the day when electricity is still out. Black plastic is used to provide privacy, generate heat, or when applied correctly, create the illusion that no one is home or that there is no electricity being used at a residence. The latter is important if you find yourself in a situation in which criminals are targeting those with resources the general public does not have. This technique was used extensively during WWII to reduce target visibility to enemy bombers at night. The use of **black-out window coverings** could keep unwanted visitors from being drawn to your home. Black-out coverings can be pulled up or removed during the day to allow light in if you wish. If used during winter, this additional layer can help insulate windows and keep in heat. As with the other types of window coverings, pre-cut and labeled plastic makes it quick and easy to apply. Better to have it and not need it, then need it and not have it.

Be on the lookout for downed power lines, debris, and branches or limbs. LED lights that clip to the bill of a cap or hat are helpful because the beam of light moves as you turn your head. This hands-free approach is a great back up in case you drop your handheld light or need to carry something or someone. The only negative is the unintentional high-beaming of people around you. It takes thought and coordination to avoid this when working closely with other people in the dark. This is important in recovery efforts right after damaging storms such as tornados and hurricanes.

It is good to have a **map** of your town, metro area and state in your **Storm Response Kit.** In the case of tornados, the landscape can become so altered that it may be difficult to navigate by sight alone. A map can help you fill in gaps and missing street sign names. If you have a detailed map of your area or that of a loved one, you are better able to navigate as you respond. Consider adding physical landmarks on the route to important locations within your SA. If street signs are missing or roads are obscured by debris, some of the landmarks may remain and orient you as to your location. This can help you find what you are looking for.

Other Reasons to Shelter in Place

Storm and power outage preparations incorporate the basic steps needed for all emergencies. Food, water, every day hygiene items, and over the counter medicines are the foundation of any good preparedness plan. In addition to these are less common, but still important, emergencies which may require you to shelter in place. These situations require additional supplies and planning.

Consider preparing for an outbreak of communicable disease and the possibility of airborne contaminates such as smoke drift from wildfires or even the discharge of biological weapons.

While severe weather is the most common reason for sheltering in place, there are other scenarios to be prepared for. Most of the supplies for these situations are items we use on a regular basis. If you never need these supplies in an emergency, they will still be used as you rotate them into your pantry. As a result, being prepared to shelter in place provides peace of mind while requiring little that may remained unused.

Medical Isolation

Preparing to care for your family in the event of a local outbreak of epidemic disease is a vital, but often overlooked aspect of preparedness. In our modern culture, we are generally unfamiliar with home nursing practices. Modern medicine makes it rare that we are ill for a prolonged time outside of the hospital setting. The ease of travel, changes in social culture, and the availability of assisted living centers has drastically decreased the number of multi-generational households in western countries. The result is a loss of home nursing skills being passed down as families care for their sick and elderly. Simple, but vital skills such as giving a bed bath or an occupied bed change are now the domain of professional care givers.

Not all reasons for medical isolation are the stuff off Hollywood blockbusters. While epidemic or pandemic outbreak of communicable disease can occur, so can influenza or head lice at your child's school. Whether you wish to avoid illness or *your* family are the ones sick, it is good to have the needed medical supplies on hand. I will not go into everything you should stock up on because there are already many great books and articles on this topic. Instead, I will share some tips not frequently discussed. Some of these are a bit graphic due to medical conditions you may need to address. Despite our general aversion to discussing toileting and other bodily functions, they are part of life and must be addressed.

I have made buying items that we need most a top priority. When it comes to illness, the top priority purchases are pain/fever reducers, anti -nausea liquid, anti-diarrheal pills, toilet paper, and tissues. In previous generations, the inability to control fever and dehydration claimed many lives. Febrile seizures, brain damage, and kidney failure can often be avoided with the appropriate use of over the counter (OTC) medication. Most of these remedies are less than six dollars and should be stocked up on during sales. Don't forget to check expiration dates and select bottles with the newest dates. Sales are often designed to clear out medication nearing expiration. Looking toward the back of the shelf can often yield medication that lasts longer. Remember that medications are sensitive to heat and sunlight which decrease their effectiveness and shorten their lifespan. Unless otherwise indicated, store medications in cool, dark locations.

After you have those basics, consider adding cold and allergy medication, cough suppressants and expectorants, vitamin supplements, diaper cream and topical muscle pain preparations. Also store various preparations for constipation. Changes in diet, immobility from being in bed, and many pain medications can cause constipation. Fiber supplements, laxatives, glycerin suppositories and enemas can ease discomfort and help avoid serious medical problems. By storing several options, you can respond to the issue regardless of the degree of severity, cause, and age of the patient.

When possible, stock items that serve multiple purposes. Petroleum jelly, for example, is inexpensive and has many uses during illness. It can be used on chapped lips due to mouth breathing due to congestion. It can also be used beneath the nose and on the bottom to prevent chaffing from frequent wiping. Both are very tender locations that cause serious discomfort if allowed to become raw. It also moisturizes and waterproofs skins. This is especially important during dry, cold weather. Prevention is the name of the game, especially when outside medical attention is not available or you simply wish to avoid additional exposure to disease.

Always use a clean spoon or wooden craft stick to remove an application of salve or petroleum jelly from the jar to prevent contaminating the remaining contents. **No double dipping**. If the applicator touches a wound or other unsanitary surface, use a new one for additional application. Craft (Popsicle) sticks can be bought in boxes of 100 or more very cheaply. They are also good for mixing small amounts of ingredients together. Compounding mixtures is more common when you use herbal or home remedies such as adding herbs to a dose of honey or making a small batch of diaper cream. Mixing in a dosing cup helps insure you measure correctly and that you can get all the mix out of the cup.

Medical Equipment

There are many home diagnostic tools you can purchase to help monitor the health of your family. **Otoscopes**, for viewing in the ears, are readily available. These are especially helpful with young children who are often unable to articulate the source of their distress. There are many holistic remedies for ear infections if you cannot get to a doctor. Purchase a good **stethoscope** and a **blood pressure monitor**. While electronic monitors are fine, remember to also store and learn to use a manual version. If your electronic monitor breaks, the electricity goes out, runs out of batteries or is damaged by an EMP, you can still monitor blood pressure. Practice regularly to become comfortable using them and familiar with your family member's vitals. Speaking of vital signs, don't forget **thermometers**. If possible, store a few old-fashion, mercury thermometers in case your electronic versions are not an option. These are increasingly difficult to find due to concerns over mercury hazards and the convenience of digital versions. New to the public market are **pulse oximeters**. These are the small devices placed on a finger to read your blood oxygen level and count your heart beats per minute. Once only available to doctors and hospitals, these helpful tools are now affordable and easy to use. I recently checked prices and found they ranged from $20 - $60 for basic models. They can be purchased at most pharmacies or online. If you can operate a clothes pin, you can use a pulse oximeter. This device can tell you a person's pulse and the percentage of oxygen they are getting as they breathe. Both details are important to the understanding and treatment of someone who is ill.

Learn how to use these tools and what is normal for various members of your family. When someone is ill, you will be better able to discuss their condition with medical professionals or to care for them when no help is available. It is smart to make a folder or notebook with a page for each person in the family. Take their vitals and record them with the date, time and whether they were resting, engaging in regular activities, or working hard when the vitals were taken. Over time, this will give you an idea of what is normal for each person. Teach as many family members, as are old enough, how to take vitals. These measurements of baseline health are: temperature, heart rate per minute, blood pressure, and oxygen level. Many of these factors are dependent on health and fitness level. Learning what is healthy and what your numbers are is a great way to see where you can improve your health. As you work on weight loss, fitness and stamina, and stress management, you can see the results in your vital statistics. This is a good source of positive re-enforcement.

It is important to protect essential medical equipment from possible electro-magnetic damage caused by solar flares or EMP weapons. Create small **Faraday cages** for your medical devices including blood pressure monitors, glucometers, insulin pumps, digital thermometers, pulse oximeters, and a few small calculators for measurement conversions. Be sure to follow reputable instructions for EMP proofing these supplies. Excellent instructions are available online and in book form. We use large popcorn tins for medical and personal electronic devices. These are easier to keep indoors than larger metal trash cans or drums. Indoor storage allows for temperature control of sensitive devices.

In addition to medicine and diagnostic devices, think of things you might need if you had to treat a prolonged illness or injury. This is the gritty stuff no one wants to talk about. It's a little gross, but it's the truth. In the movies, when the hero gets shot, he wakes up to find he is being cared for by the pretty young widow. Next comes my favorite line. "How long was I out?" The response usually varies from a few days to weeks. I have never seen a movie or book, for that matter, that dared address the obvious issues of **feeding, hygiene, or elimination**. (Yes, being a prepper has ruined many movies for me.) For the purposes of preparedness, consider what a home nurse would need to do just to address those three issues.

After purchasing and learning to use those items, focus on supplies to treat the reason the person is bed ridden. In the interest of realism, consider doing this without electricity. If you are rendering prolonged patient care, chances are the situation is really bad. This usually means no power. It could be overwhelming to say the least.

Before discussing the supplies, you should stockpile, I would like to share some observations gleaned from family experience. Sharing what we have learned, allows others to benefit from the lessons of our family's medical trials. There is nothing quite like firsthand experience to help you acquire empathy and wisdom. Here are some things we have learned about prolonged recoveries that may help you.

- Staying in bed for more than a day or two can be physically uncomfortable, even painful. We all think we would stay in bed for days if we could, but you would quickly find it's not as comfy as you think. Our bodies were designed to operate upright and to move. Sleep was meant to be a five to ten-hour activity that recharges us for the next day. I was amazed how quickly a person becomes stiff and sore from being in bed or confined to a chair. One of the first things to learn about and store supplies for, is patient positioning. This is especially true if the person is unable to communicate for some reason. Small pillows or bolsters for relieving pressure can be placed under the knees and under the ankle, just above the heel, in the small of the back, and in the curve of the neck. Suitable pillows can be found at thrift stores or made inexpensively. Consider pillow cases to prevent soiling and cross contamination. If it is to be used in an area that may become wet, slip the pillow into a plastic bag before the pillow case. Use sacks from your stash of plastic shopping bags for smaller pillows and loosely tie the bag.

- Prolonged inactivity causes skin irritation and can lead to pressure breakdown of the skin commonly known as bed sores. Heels, knees, the sacrum and tailbone are the most common sites. The pressure of simply lying in bed can cause pressure breakdown faster if the patient cannot shift position on their own or if they have impaired sensation in an area. Once an area has become pink and warm to the touch, it is difficult to prevent damage. Frequent position changes, pressure relief measures, and daily inspection of skin can reduce the likelihood of ulcers developing.

- A bedside commode is a handy piece of equipment to own. When an individual is injured or seriously ill, getting to the restroom in time can be difficult. Consider placing a bed side commode near the bed. This can prevent further injury, reduce the need for clean-up of an accident, and limit the spread of germs outside the patient's room. The toilet has a removable bucket which can be emptied, washed and replaced as needed. This is also handy under normal circumstances for episodes of severe flu and post-operative recovery.

Home Health and Nursing Supplies

- Walker, cane, and crutches
- Extra towels and wash cloths
- Fitted and flat bed sheets for bed
- Bed sheets for use as first aid supplies
- Ace bandages, ankle braces, splints, slings
- Bed pan, fracture pan and urinal
- Disposable under garments
- Skin protecting/barrier cream
- Disinfecting and deodorizing spray
- Sanitary napkins – panty liners and maxi pads
- Urinary incontinent pads for men and women
- Wipes, no-rinse hair care and bath supplies
- Some type of in bed hair washing basin
- Ointment for dry and cracked skin, bruises and wounds
- Washable and disposable under pads for seats and bedding
- Small plastic bags for biohazard waste (shopping bags)
- Larger trash bags for bagging soiled linen and clothing

Civil Unrest

Another reason you may need to shelter in place is civil unrest. Protests, riots, and violent outbursts by citizens have become common place in the last few years. Whether it's political, racial, religious, or gang related, public violence seems to be on the rise. Having the ability to stay home until danger has passed is a responsible goal. Many episodes are short, one day events, while others have stretched into nightly rioting and looting for days. Keeping well stocked, especially during storm seasons will make it easier to stay off the road and away from trouble that can arise in business districts.

In addition to keeping well stocked, keeping up with **current events** can help you prepare for incidents of civil unrest. Polarizing events increase the likelihood of protesters and acts of violence. In addition to trusted televised news sources, search for device apps and online sites to refer to use on the go.

Food Preparation and Preservation

Although most of the instances in which you might need to shelter in place are brief, some scenarios could last weeks or months. Every household should have at least two people who know how to prepare and preserve food in different ways. Teaching an older child to assist a parent is a great way to accomplish this. Involving this child in meal preparations and in activities such as baking or canning provides opportunities for bonding and fun in addition to gaining valuable skills. Knowing many techniques gives you flexibility and options. Consider learning about the following food preparation and preservation skills:

- Dehydrating with and without electricity
- Water bath and pressure canning
- Various methods of camp & solar cooking
- Indigenous methods of processing and drying food
- Basic understanding of meal planning for good nutrition
- Use and care of cast iron ware
- Methods for preparing and preserving game

These skills sets are highlighted because they represent knowledge that can help sustain life in your home or at a bug out location. If you are on your own or separated from those in the Food Prep and Preservation Skill Group, you would still be able to care for your family. These basic skills are also essential for putting up garden and bulk produce purchases and fish and wild game that add to your food supply under normal circumstances.

CHAPTER 21

Bug-Out Locations

f possible, every Survival Alliance should have at least one preselected location to evacuate to if your primary residence is unsafe or becomes indefensible. This location should at least be prepared for communal living and be stocked with food, water, and medical supplies. If this is not currently feasible, look at the possibility of combining households within the group. Do some members have homes suitable to hosting another family or more during an emergency. If so, coordinate plans for evacuation. What items are realistic to leave at their home? Which items will you need to bring? Sheltering in place in groups provides additional security and hands to help with tasks.

Those with long-term concerns can develop accommodations for people and animals in advance. These can include prepared tent platforms, simple cabins, sheds and stalls and hutches of various types. Consider preparing garden beds and greenhouses for raising crops and storage areas for feed and supplies. These are some of the things to consider when evaluating property for a bug out location:

- How defensible is this property? A Google Earth view of the proposed property can give you a valuable view and help you plan SA security and defense. Print aerial views and use for planning. List the ways onto the property, proximity to roads and other property boundaries. How long are the boundaries? How many guards are needed to patrol them?
- How accessible is it? Are the roads that lead to the proposed location publicly maintained roads? This can be important because private roads may fall into disrepair making them sloppy in bad weather. On the other hand, private roads are not as well-known and have less traffic.
- Find out if the roads are prone to flooding, snow drift, are on the snow route, on the city evacuation route, or if the roads are paved. The answers to these questions will help you decide which route to take and even if the location is a smart choice. Imagine your town or the neighboring large city being evacuated. What might that look like?
- Where will the traffic flow in relation to your property? What problems might that cause? Can your SA cope with those issues? Are there major roads nearby? In addition to evacuation traffic, consider which roads refugees may use to search for food, water, and supplies. Gangs may travel these roads looking for their next victims. Like rats off a sinking ship, bigger cities will empty into smaller, neighboring towns and rural landscape. The closer you are to major roads, the harder it will be to defend from large groups. An excellent picture of this is illustrated in the beginning of the novel <u>One Second After.</u>
- Who lives around you? Take note of who owns the neighboring land and learn a little about them. Knowing your neighbors in advance of a crisis can tell you if they can they be counted on to help or could they be part of your problem? If they do not live there or it is owned by a business such as an oil or natural gas site, how often do they visit? Many of these sites lease cattle grazing to ranchers. If cattle are on the site, the owners will come to check on them periodically.
- Is there a source of water on it? Rivers, lakes, ponds, wells, cisterns, swimming pools and stock tanks are common sources of water which can be filtered or boiled for drinking and cooking. Aerial views of the area will let you know if there is water on neighboring properties. Google Earth can provide this overhead perspective. Depending on whether the land is occupied, you can make use of the water in an emergency. If it is occupied, knowledge of their resource can position you to negotiate and barter.

- Is there enough open space for growing food? If you intend to grow your food, you will need open space that is not in the path of flood water or pooling water. Observe the land during and right after heavy rain. Note where the water sheds and gathers. Write this down so you don't plant, house animals or people on these sites.

- Is there enough land to sustain grazing animals? If you intend to raise larger livestock, you will need open acreage for grazing and cutting hay for winter. Depending on the number, goats, sheep, and pigs can free range on partial wooded lots. Cattle and horses require open pastures of good quality grass. Fields are usually a mixture of weeds, brush and grass. Goats and donkeys are less picky, and can thrive on a variety of plants. Cattle and horses require grasses. Consider planting grass seed to encourage the production of better pastures. Grass can be mowed and stored as hay for winter months.

- What is the annual rainfall for the area? Although this can change, finding out the average rainfall for the past 10 years. This number can help you decide if this location is good for gardening and livestock.

- If possible, use a topographical map to determine the lay of the land. This information can help you determine if there is a good location for a runoff pond. This information can also be used to locate buildings where they will be safe from high water if you cannot visit during or right after heavy rain.

- Is this area prone to severe seasonal weather such as blizzards or tornados? Planting trees to provide wind breaks for animals or housing can provide protection from driving winds and snow. This process is slow and takes time. The sooner you start, the sooner these trees can be assets to your property.

Consider the possibility of the bug out location not being owned by anyone in the group. Basically, consider evacuating to a well-researched property with little chance of interaction with the owners. Although not ideal, having selected a place to evacuate to, even if it isn't your property, is better than staying somewhere that is not safe. If choosing this option, remember that you are **trespassing** if you enter without permission. Only use this option if there is a true break down of law and order and be prepared for others who may do the same. It is an option for use only in true emergency circumstances, in which staying in your home, in town is not an option.

Depending on the situation, you may have little warning before you need to evacuate. Multiple trips to bring food, water, supplies and then family may not be possible. Having your retreat stocked with provisions in advance would be wise. If it is not safe to stock your retreat in advance, stage your bug out supplies in an orderly fashion to make loading up fast. Consider prioritizing your supplies with labels to indicate which supplies are most important. If you cannot take everything, this number system can help assure that the priority boxes go first. The supplies in my garage are labeled **BO** for **B**ug **O**ut, followed by 1,2, or 3. All BO tubs and items are together, near the garage door, for easy loading. My family knows the labeling system. If I were not home, extended family could load for me. The down side to this is that if I am not careful with my security, it would be just as easy for thieves to load my preps. You could also use false content labels such as CRAFT SUPPLIES or EXTRA SHEETS followed by 1,2, or 3 to discourage theft. Using sheets as dust covers is another way to reduce advertising your preps.

As proud as you may be of your new rotating can shelves or fully stocked safe room; do not post pictures of them on social media sites. Some of us have chosen to share our experience with others for educational purposes. We understand the possible problems this can cause and accept responsibility in the name of public service. This is not a risk everyone should take. Some preppers feel compelled to share what they know in hopes of convincing others of the need to be prepared. Many of us have taken steps to mitigate the risks of public disclosure to ourselves and our groups.

If you are wondering who cares about your preps, right now the answer is generally, no one. However, as soon as the economy tanks, the power goes out for a few days, or there is a disruption in deliveries to stores, you will be amazed how many people will remember you have resources and be on your doorstep. Most of them will be folks who told you that you were nuts and spent their money on frivolous things. Your home will be an anthill to the proverbial grasshoppers who know about your preps. What will you do then?

Consider keeping fuel at your retreat or packed for sheltering in place. Be sure to factor in changing temperatures when storing gas, propane, and flammable liquids such as kerosene. Charcoal is a safe fuel source for cooking. You can use it to Dutch oven cook. Store a chart that indicates how many briquettes are needed above and below for specific recipes. Charcoal frequently goes on sale after special occasions such as the Fourth of July, during football season, and at the end of summer. Keep it dry by using plastic storage pails and tubs with lids. Lighter fluid is often on sale at the same time. Consult labels, the internet, and your local fire department for safety guidelines. Another form of fuel storage is keeping your gas tank at least half full. Make it a habit to top off when you stop for groceries at super stores with gas stations or if you stop at convenience stores regularly. If there is an evacuation or emergency of any kind, lines at gas stations will be long and potentially dangerous. If debit machines aren't working or are limiting withdrawals, mugging and robbery will be a danger.

In addition to food, water and medical supplies, cache **building materials** and a tool kit, old fashion hand tools, repair and maintenance supplies for shelters, out buildings, outhouses, etc. if such are not already on the property. Consider precutting lumber and drilling pilot holes for screws and long nails. Instructions can be stored in freezer bags, along with hardware, and bundled in a tarp. Use a permanent marker to indicate the project in the bundle and store flat in a dry place. If there is no electricity, the hardest part of construction is done. All that is needed is assembly. Also, store several screw drivers and hammers needed to allow others to help with construction. The projects you choose depend on your SA type and where you live.

Construction Kits Examples

- Outhouse
- Shower/changing stall
- Chicken tractor
- Rabbit/chicken hutch
- Simple shed style sleeping quarters

Construction sites are great places to get wood for these types of projects. The needed pieces aren't generally very big, making construction scraps perfect. Be sure to contact the developer or general contractor for permission **before** taking anything – even if it is in a dumpster. While many don't care, some consider this criminal trespassing and theft. Many business owners will not allow people who are not their employees on the property for fear of liability if they become injured. I have offered an **agreement to hold harmless** when collecting construction scraps on construction sites. I explain that I would like to make a rabbit hutch (or some other small project) and that the scraps would be perfect. I have even offered to pay a modest fee for the wood or bricks if it looks like they may say no. It is still much cheaper than a trip to the local hardware store.

Another advantage is that the pieces are often more manageable than the full-size lengths sold at lumber yards or stores. For those who do not own a truck, this is a real plus. If you are using a car or van for hauling construction supplies, use a plastic tarp to protect the upholstery and carpet. I keep one in the trunk in case I am in the car when a great salvage opportunity presents itself. I also carry a blank agreement to hold harmless in my glovebox. I recommend finding examples online to print. If you have an opportunity to speak with a foreman or owner, you are ready. Leave your name and phone number with the form if they need to check with someone before giving permission.

Being prepared means putting in the effort before an emergency to decrease the impact on life and property. It becomes a way of thinking and acting, but the rewards of peace of mind and safety are well worth it.

CHAPTER 22
Survival Alliance Communication Plans and SOPs

t is important to develop a **Communication Plan** to account for all the members in your Alliance during and after emergencies. The first method of communication should be phone and then internet. This keeps people off roads that may not be safe and may prevent more rescues for fire, police and ambulance workers. A current roster of SA members is essential to doing this. Some groups may not be comfortable keeping such a roster on a computer, while others are. If you are concerned about membership information being compromised, have members fill out copies of the SA Contact form, in Appendix 1. Keep them in a secure location. Use these forms to create handwritten lists, organized by location, to perform welfare checks. Make photo copies of lists for use in emergency situations. Periodically remind members to update their contact information. Changes in home or work address and phone numbers should be reported as soon as possible.

For the sake of convenience, consider dividing members into groups based on geographic location. Assign the nearest SGL (skill group leader) to conduct the welfare checks in that area if there are concerns about member safety. Living in the same general area makes it more likely that they will be familiar with low water crossings, snow routes, alternate routes if roads are impassable, and resources available in the area. If members are spread out, it is important to share this type of information. If you have a large group, consider using multiple SGLs.

Using local maps, create shaded areas indicating the geographical zones that your membership is divided into. Color code for quick visual reference and assign a number or letter to each for written and verbal reference. Local Chambers of Commerce and Better Business Bureaus often have free maps available to residents. All members should have a current copy of this information. Schedule periodic review and updates for all maps. This will allow for the addition of new roads, changes in road condition, or access and long- term construction projects to be added to SA maps.

SA Communication Plans should also have guidelines for groups texts within the group, as well as the use of alerts from local and national weather and news apps. Discuss which apps you will use to standardize the information members are acting on. If leadership determines that information requires a change in the SA Alert status, this change can be issued through group text and ham radio in the absence of phone service. Consider standardizing phone type and apps within the group. Some features and apps are not universal. A good example are the differences between Android and Apple products. If you do not standardize the operating systems, be sure the features and apps you use work on both.

If the event is severe and there is no response from some members, it may be necessary to physically check on them. Once you and your family are safe, contact the police or fire department with your concerns. Give them the name, address, and phone number of the member you have lost contact with. If there is any information about their property such as gates, locks, guard dogs, or the location of their storm shelter that would be helpful, forward that as well. If you are told that it will be some time before officials can check on the members in question, you may decide to do it yourself. The decision to do so should be made only after careful consideration of the dangers you may encounter and your ability to deal with them. Discretion is the better part of valor. If you end up needing rescue as well, both of you will wait until authorities get to you. Meanwhile, your family will do without your help and reassurance.

When performing welfare checks for fellow SA members or neighbors, be sure to take appropriate supplies and equipment. Keeping a backpack or duffle bag packed for this purpose is a good idea. It is important to have response gear appropriate to the types of events you may encounter. Add seasonal items, such as a blanket, an umbrella, snow grips for your shoes, and sand or cat litter for snow traction. Be sure to switch out seasonal items each year. Doing this when you change your smoke detector batteries and update group rosters makes it easy to remember. Basic **CERT** bags have well thought out contents. Each item serves multiple purposes for common accidents and disasters. They can be purchased online or duplicated using the list below.

Basic CERT Bag Content List

- 1 hard hat
- 15' pry bar
- Metal whistle
- Duct tape
- Caution tape
- Knee pads
- Gas shut off tool
- N95 dust mask
- 12 hour light stick
- N95 particle mask
- Large mayday solar blanket
- D size flashlight /batteries
- 3 mayday water pouches
- Heavy duty work gloves
- Vented safety goggles

Recommended Basic First Aid Kit

Nitrile medical gloves
4x4 non-stick and gauze pads
bandages in assorted sizes
Sam splint/ reusable splint
ace wrap and self-cling wrap
sterile irrigation saline
Israeli battle or pressure dressing
triple antibiotic – single use pkts
small spiral notebook and pen

Caution: Good Samaritan laws only cover treatment that you have been trained to administer. Get trained.

After you have secured your location, you can consider moving out to help others or attempt to get home. Before leaving your location, be sure you have done a safety assessment. Is it safe for you to leave? This information is part of the **size up** process taught in **CERT**. Before leaving look for information on road conditions and possible closings. If you have cell phone service, it should be policy to relay your progress during welfare checks, as well as general home and business damage seen on route that can be used by the group for planning purposes. Contact your SGL when you leave for and arrive at your destination. If you have not called to report your progress on the welfare check at the agreed upon time, they will call you. If you do not answer, they will assume you are incapacitated and need assistance as well. Upon making contact with the people being checked on, report their status to the appropriate SA leader.

Standard Operating Procedures

Another form of planning, necessary for a successful Survival Alliance, is a set of standard operating practices, or **SOPs**. These are the protocols for important activities and responses to various situations. They serve as guidelines to ensure that individuals and the group act using approved methods which are familiar to other members. This allows for continuity within the group, and helps everyone knows what is expected. It is also a means of increasing safety and cooperation between members. When it comes to certain situations, there is no *your* way or *my* way, but instead, the SOP way.

There are several categories into which SOPs can be divided. This will vary depending on the variety of events your SA is prepping for. Generally, you will have **administrative**, **security**, **defensive**, and **disaster response** protocols. I would recommend the following topics be covered by an SOP:

- Vetting of perspective members to include any qualifications, disqualifiers, and introducing candidates to the SA, requirements for admission and expulsion

- Handling and dispersal of any money
- Membership, medical, training, and inventory records with related privacy and security issues
- Home and retreat location security standards for prevention and threat response
- Vehicles – equipment and readiness requirements
- Communication – methods, security, and instances in which specific information will be sent, who is authorized to issue the various forms of alerts or safety messages, channels or bands to be broadcast or any code or encryption used
- Evacuation routes and rendezvous points, including alternates and conditions under which such would be used
- Defense of individual and communal homes and property under various circumstances, expectations of members in those circumstances, specific plans or techniques to be utilized in various scenarios

If your SA wants to be prepared to evacuate and set up at an alternate location or rendering aid in your community, consider adding:

- Creation of duty roster for setting up camp to include putting up tents or building shelters, creation or set up of latrines, securing water and fire wood supply, maintenance of fires, meals, and security.
- Roster of individuals who are qualified and able to perform various post disaster duties, response bag list with add-on lists for specialty tasks, protocol for setting up a command center, coordinating with local authorities, set up of triage and treatment areas, and morgue if needed. Refer to CERT manual for best practices.
- Map or list of addresses in SA neighborhoods with any demographic information such as number in household, names, approximate ages, special needs etc. This can be used to conduct searches and record welfare check results

Speaking of checking on neighbors; **get to know your neighbors**. As a society, we have allowed ourselves to become disconnected from the people who live around us. Even casual relationships with the people on your street can create a sense of community and cooperation. This connection can in turn lead to being more watchful and proactive on one another's behalf. If you need to do a welfare check in your neighborhood, you are much safer if you are recognized and trusted.

There are lots of ways to get know your neighbors. If you belong to a home owner's association or neighborhood watch program you can use meetings and gatherings as opportunities to socialize. Take advantage of opportunities to serve in leadership positions, on committees, and patrols for access to more detailed information. Even simple acts like waving and saying hello can start relationships and build trust. This casual contact is a great way to gather information about neighbors that can help you scout SA members. Even if you do not find good matches for your group, establishing a rapport with the people who live near you is a worthwhile endeavor. As you observe people and interact with them, note those who might need extra attention or assistance. Single parents with several young children, single women living alone, the elderly, and those with disabilities are examples. Consider checking on these households prior to serious weather events, after power outages and storms, and if the power goes out in extreme heat or cold. This type of service blesses the giver and recipient, and creates safer neighborhoods. Other benefits include:

- **Recognition** of need- Knowing who is most vulnerable and what they need most can help you effectively prioritize the **order** in which you serve neighbors.
- **Prioritization** of assistance - Obviously, those with the fewest physical, social, and financial resources should be checked on first. In some instances, minutes are the difference between life and death as in cases of hypothermia, heat stroke, heart attacks, and need to evacuate to safety.
- **Decreasing fraud and theft** - If people pull together within a neighborhood and assist one another, they are less likely to need help from strangers. These services are often costly and some individuals pose as aid workers to gain access to homes and property to take advantage of the homeowner.
- **Increased response time** - After disasters, it is not uncommon for municipal responders to be overwhelmed. This shortage of manpower results in increased response time to calls for help. State and federal aid are often delayed, so, it is

important to be prepared to fend for yourself for a bit. FEMA requests that citizens be prepared to meet their own needs for seventy-two hours after a disaster. Could you do it? Could your family?

Security and Defense

Security and defensive practices are the most challenging unless you have several active duty or career military vets or LEOs in your group. Deciding what issues to prepare for and how they may require a great deal of research. Fortunately, there are excellent books and online resources available to help. One of our favorite resources are the many U.S. military manuals available in many libraries, online, and for sale in print. Some of the topics you should cover are:

- Rules of engagement for hostile individuals
- Possible standardization of firearms and ammunition
- Establish guidelines for securing individual homes and property
- Guidelines for assisting friends, neighbors, and strangers
- Guard duty responsibilities, shift length. and areas to be covered
- Post disaster size up and securing of home, property or neighborhood
- Establishment of consequences for violation of SA regulations

There are many other topics that can and should be covered under the heading of Security and Defense. Which ones you create SOPs for will depend on the type of Survival Alliance you have. Brain storming with group members can be a great way to work out which issues are relevant to your alliance. Prepper and disaster fiction can provide scenarios upon which you base these discussions. Take individual situations and talk about the how the group might react. Policy and guidelines can evolve as you seriously discuss threat prevention and response. Keep in mind the temperament and skills of your members as you develop your SOPs. It does no good to create a plan of action that few, if any, can carry out. Once you have agreed upon these policies, hold training events to familiarize members with the how they should handle those situations.

CHAPTER 23

Survival Alliance Alert System

To establish a uniform state of preparedness, consider instituting an alert system. This standardized method can quickly and efficiently convey information to your SA regarding their state of readiness. This is especially well suited to cell phone messaging. It is important to designate a few people within the Alliance who may issue alerts or make changes in the alert status. Consider the SA Leader and one other person. If one or both are unable for any reason, they can select someone to serve in their place temporarily. Establishing a chain of command will eliminate confusion regarding who is in charge.

All members should be encouraged to pass information that has bearing on the alert status to those who issue the alerts. There is so much information out there that the more people watching, the better. Limiting the number of people who can actually issue alerts ensures that information has been vetted and SA leadership has approved the alert. Your system can have as many levels as you want. This can be a number, color or word designation indicating a specific condition. It should also indicate specific action to be taken by SA members. Examples are:

The Number System

Level 1 – Normal – maintain regular routine and preparedness

Level 2 – Slightly elevated vigilance – Follow trusted news sources

Level 3 – Significant possible threat – Keep cash on hand, top off perishables and basic preps and stay tuned to trusted news sources.

Level 4 – Imminent threat – Prepare to shelter in place or bug-out (depending on whichever is most appropriate). Consider removing money from bank, topping off gas supplies, buying any supplies/food needed for prolonged event, purchase ammo if needed. Begin home security measures.

Level 5 – Bug-out or shelter in place. All defensive measures in place.

The Color System

Green – All clear – Normal routine

Yellow – Possible threat identified – follow issue closely

Orange – Threat impact verified – Top off food, medical, fuel and technical supply. Prepare to shelter in place/ bug-out. Activate appropriate defensive measures and stay tuned to trusted news sources.

Red - Prepare for imminent threat impact (weather, economic, criminal, military) Implement safety measures for home, property, and family.

After you have decided what type of alert system you want to use, consider who will be issuing the alerts. This may be a designated individual or anyone within a selected group. The important thing is that there are guidelines for who can issue an alert and under what circumstances. Consider if your group wants the decision to issue certain alerts to be approved by anyone else in the group first or if the issuer has sole discretion. I would suggest that this can vary depending on the type of alert. Some information will change the readiness level, while others will not. Consider prefacing group texts with a word to indicate the type of text that follows. In this way, members can see the urgency of the text in a glance. We use **Alert** for urgent information and **Notice** for important, but not urgent. You could choose a three-word designation system that uses **Urgent** as the highest priority messages, followed by **Alert** and **Notice**. Regardless of which words you use, be consistent and sparing in the issuance of group messages. These words can also be used with verbal communications such as ham radio and voicemail.

In addition to message status code words, choose a word or phrase that indicates the **inability of the sender to speak/text freely or ITSF**. This could be used if the conversation could be recorded, overheard, or read. Examples are work or social situations where privacy cannot be guaranteed or brevity is essential. Agree on a word, number or variation of the ITSF word itself to indicate you are ok, just not able to communicate freely. If the safe word is not used, the reader is to assume the reason you cannot communicate freely is due to a situation of a dangerous nature. Your word or phrase should be conversational to eliminate suspicion if it is read or overheard. It should be **the first thing you say** to be sure it is received in the event of disruption. All members of the family and SA should be familiar with these words or phrases.

Clear, concise communication is critical to SA success. Practice working your ITSF word into conversation or texting to find a routine you are comfortable with. Doing this with the people you are most likely to contact in an emergency is a great way to familiarize them with this technique. Be sure that you tell them you are about to practice this *prior* to training. You can even say or type **PRACTICE** at the beginning of the exercise. Get in the habit of indicating you have received and understood communications by using a word such as OK, understood, or roger. Wilco, short for will comply, is a great way to indicate that you agree to whatever action was requested and that you intend to do it. Remember to say or type **PRACTICE OVER** at the end. Doing this within a created scenario can help you work out what to say and how to say it. We chose our security words and phrases while doing such an exercise. Pretending you were in a sensitive situation and that you might have your conversation monitored helps find ways to work in the **ITSF** code word/phrase. Remember to indicate hostile or normal circumstances. You don't want your wife calling the police and have them GPS your phone if you can't talk because you are in a meeting, but needed to tell her something urgent.

Group Texts

Your SA can issue as many group messages as you feel is appropriate. I would caution against issuing messages that are not time sensitive. Also, be cautious in the use of URGENT as a designation. Overuse of messaging or inflating the importance of information can lead to members ignoring or not checking messages frequently. It boils down to maintaining credibility. The key is to be sure to indicate the priority level of the text and to not over use texts. If you issue group messages about every little thing, the important messages may not be heeded. Here are some of the types of alerts your SA could issue:

- **Weather** alerts in conjunction with approved news sources
- **Economic** news that can impact members, with data, time frames, and sources of the information and possible member response
- **Political** actions with direct, imminent effect on citizens such as rallies, protests, important votes or elections, and legislation changes along with possible implications for SA members
- **Criminal** activity such as prison escapes, rioting, volatile protests, looting, social media chatter regarding civil unrest and disruption of events, business, or flow of traffic or vetted inside information regarding any dangerous activity

- **Medical** information regarding spread of disease due to epidemic, pandemic, water supply, food supply, biological weapons, or damage to transport or storage containers of hazardous substances
- **Religious** information and opportunities of interest to your SA (if your group is faith based) such as special speakers, or events that have scriptural significance

Along with status changes, develop actions to be taken. Decide if these actions are suggestions for members or are mandatory expectations. You could institute a combination of both types. A good reason for some or all expectations being mandatory is the actions will produce **guaranteed** additional fuel, food, water and security. If thoughtfully issued, alert status changes, with accompanying actions, could yield supplies and safety responses critical to the well-being of the group. After changes in group alert status, hold after action reviews with members. These can be conducted by one person or divided between SA leadership. Record which members were able act on the recommendations and what they did. Some members may be in situations where they cannot leave. Others may be free to act on the recommendations given. Finding out, for example, that a member did purchase the requested amount of gas plus 10 gallons, may offset another member who was at work and told they were being held over due to weather etc.

After all members have reported, the results should be reviewed by leadership to determine how effectively the group responded to the alert status change. Families should conduct their own reviews to include children. Parents know which of their children can handle what information. Like fire drills, these reviews serve to remind children of age appropriate responses to potential danger and teach them to be proactive. Preparation to serve others can be taught as well, depending on the situation. Teaching children to take in information, anticipate the impact on them, choose steps to prepare, and then go about their life, is a vital life skill and a blessing. Avoiding topics, you find stressful, is a disservice to them. If they encounter emergency situations while away from you, they will not have the skills to respond appropriately. The trick is to give information without overwhelming them. Periodic drills are smart ways to do this. Since the danger is not real, they can focus on the decision-making part. Over time, these responses will become automatic and come naturally, even under real circumstances.

Once you have created your SOPs, develop a handbook or manual for group members to refer to. Having responses and expectations in print makes it much easier to remember and review with family. Remind members that the SOP book is privileged information and should not to be shared outside the group. It should not be left lying about where it could be easily found as it may contain personal information about other members and specific plans for evacuation and defense. If you generated it on a computer, be sure that that computer is secured. Laptops make this much easier and are portable, making them great for use during meetings and training.

Visual Alerts

Another way to communicate without electricity is flags. These can be used to indicate the status of your family and property to members driving by, watching from a distance with binoculars, or if you do not want contact with others due to illness (yours or outsiders). If there is no phone contact, a flag indicating all is well, posted where it can be seen from the road, enables the individual checking on members to move on to the next home. A flag indicating assistance is required can bring help quickly.

You can also use actual signal flags to signal to aircraft if you want to really expand your communication ability. These same signals can be used to communicate with rescuers you know are observing you from a distance due to debris or other hazards. Boy Scout and military manuals are excellent sources of ideas for using flags. You can also create a color system that is exclusive to your group. These can be easy to make or purchased in a variety of sizes.

Regardless of the methods you use to keep in touch, good communication within your SA is essential to the groups success. Build in back-ups to every method to ensure you can communicate under any circumstance. If you do, you will have the peace of mind that comes from knowing you can share information, ask for and receive help, and be ready for whatever happen next.

CHAPTER 24
Family and Survival Alliance Operational Security

Good family and SA OPSEC (operational security) planning and training should involve members of all ages. As you create response plans and rules, consider the needs and capacity of each age group. Design explanations and training that take these factors into account. Be careful how you introduce information. You want to instill confidence not overwhelm, create fear, and paranoia.

Once you have selected rules, plans of action, and standard operating procedures (SOPs), it is important to educate your family or group. Discuss general and regional preparedness topics. Explain why some things cannot be shared outside the group, but do so with care. The following example illustrates the danger of not tailoring information to the developmental stage of the child.

A family works to gain a year's worth of food and other provisions. They have a family communication plan and practice various camp and survival skills. The parents have always told the children that their preps and drills are not to be discussed outside of the family and their like -minded friends that they practice with. One Monday, a teacher asks their seven-year old daughter what she did that weekend. The little girl fidgeted uncomfortably in her seat and stared down at her shoes. When pressed by her teacher she simply said, "It's a secret. Daddy told me never to talk about it." Concerned, the teacher arranged to have the school counselor speak with the child. When pressed by the counselor for information about what happened over the weekend the little girl began to cry and said that she feared she would be punished for telling. Child protective services were contacted and several tense hours passed before the parents were reached and the misunderstanding cleared up.

Rules regarding privacy and security must be explained in an **age appropriate** way to prevent problems. After explaining something, it's smart to have the child repeat **their understanding** of what you just said. This is different than saying, "Repeat what I just said." Asking them to share their understanding of what you said may take a little coaxing. A series of questions and the use of hypothetical scenarios can test their comprehension. Be patient and review the information periodically to reinforce the concepts.

There are many methods of keeping your personal and SA supplies and plans private. Some methods are very low tech and others are very sophisticated. These measures can be actions that cost nothing, items that are inexpensive, or technology that is very expensive. What tactics you use will vary depending upon the type and size of your SA. Here are some examples by category:

Securing Home/Out Buildings

- **Pad locks** - Color code or number keys but do not label. in case they are lost or stolen they cannot be traced back to you or to specific items. Color coding or numbering keys can make it faster and easier to find the one you need. Be sure to use the same system on duplicates. A disadvantage is that some types are easy to pick with proper tools and a little practice. Do your homework to select the right lock for the application.
- **Combination locks** – An advantage over pad locks is that there is no key to lose. The down side is you need to remember the combination. Combinations can be set on some types of locks. This would enable you to use the same numbers on several locks. Others come with assigned combinations which cannot be changed. Another advantage over pad locks is

that very few people can crack the combination. If these are breeched it will be due to the use of bolt cutters, blow torch or destruction of the supporting hardware.

- **Alarm systems**
- **Animals** - Guard dogs (can attack, excellent hearing and sense of smell). Guinea fowl (great noise alarms), donkeys (for protecting animals, especially against dogs, wolves, and coyotes.)
- **Camouflage** colors and netting as well as shrubs and trees to obscure visibility
- **Blackout curtains** and cardboard for temporary privacy or light suppression
- **Alarms** for windows that use batteries which can be recharged using solar power
- **Fences** – electric with solar charged battery
- **Lights** – spot lights and motion activated lights to deter animals and people
- **Perimeter alarms** such as trip wires and other improvised methods
- **Firearms** and ammunition specifically chosen for use against intruders
- **Physical barriers** such as barbed wire, fences or hedges to deter or direct human traffic. Use chicken wire or hardware cloth to enclose top over small animal enclosures to deter animal traffic. Hawks, opossums, skunks, racoons, feral cats and predators like bobcats can injure or kill livestock. Take appropriate measures if you have big cats, bears or wolves in your area.
- **Containers** – Metal and heavy plastic containers can protect food, animal feed and supplies from moisture and animals and insects.

Home or Bug Out House

- Keep grounds free of items that obstruct vision/allow intruder to get close to home without being seen and provide cover.
- Use hedges, bushes, boulders and fencing to direct the flow of people in and out of your home. These can be placed to hamper entry or slow escape,
- Have several options for cooking that create little or no smoke

Vehicles

- Lock the doors
- Have extra keys
- Locking gas caps
- Tinted glass. Sun shades
- Keep important items out of sight
- Attached and locking tool box

Food / Medical Supply Storage

- Any of the previously mentioned methods
- Log with appropriate signatures for withdrawals if under rationing
- Use of scales and measuring units for portion control verification
- Guard posted outside storage room or building if looting is a concern
- Generator powered refrigeration of temperature sensitive medication

- Generator powered refrigerator and or freezer for meat and dairy*
- Bear bag style overnight storage for freshly killed game that cannot be processed

*It is not recommended that much food inventory be dependent on refrigeration because the power required to run such devices. This food should be consumed first after power loss in case of mechanical failure or the fuel runs out or is required elsewhere.

Personal and SA Information

- Shred old notes, forms, receipts and information no longer being used.
- For groups with very strict security, use a cover club or hobby group name during unsecured or public communication. For example, "basketball practice" could be used when referring to group meetings. You could post a reminder on Facebook of basketball practice with time and place.
- Use nicknames in texts or written communications to refer to SA members if reference is being made to sensitive information. This makes it harder to associate ownership of supplies or excess food with specific people if communications are being monitored or collected for future examination.
- Do not keep pictures of members with records. Your group should know what each other looks like. This makes it easy for someone else to identify members.
- Keep pictures and serial numbers of specialty equipment that is often expensive or desirable to help with recovery if it is stolen and pawned or otherwise sold.
- Keep SA paperwork in a locked box or file. This should be portable for use during meetings or evacuation. This box should be kept in a discreet, secured location known to several members of leadership.

Security and Guard Duty

In instances where an emergency has been declared, the actual posting of guards may become necessary. This can be in anticipation of looting, disaster, or inflammatory event or in response to such. The lengths to which you go and the level of force you are willing to use, will vary depending upon the type of alliance you are in and the type of emergency you are experiencing. Deciding how you will respond should be the topic of serious, lengthy discussion.

It is important to have discussions about the situations your family and group may find themselves in. Identify any actions that are "off the table". Some individuals or groups have moral or spiritual guidelines that prohibit specific actions. Identifying these issues in advance is critical to the formation of security SOPs. Examples of potentially sensitive issues include whether to share food or supplies during emergencies, criteria for extending assistance, dealing with trespassers, use of deadly force, the use of force against women or youth, and consequences for violations of societal or SA regulations in the absence of law enforcement.

Military or law enforcement training manuals and professional training are excellent sources of information when creating threat prevention and response protocol. Identify manuals that are especially helpful and ask members to purchase copies for uniform study materials. Blogs, vlogs and video tutorials are good ways to lean new techniques and train others. Be sure to vet sources of information to be certain it represents best and current practices of any ideology or technique.

Exercises that allow participants to drill in real time or learn in simulated circumstances are essential to creating instinctive responses. Frequent **practice** leads to more accurate assessment and execution of the desired response. This is especially true of children and women who may be less comfortable with the use of force. These drills should be a mixture of verbal reviews, physical **simulations**, and response exercises. Couples and families should take advantage of **current events** to discuss appropriate responses. Putting yourself in the event being reported on and discussing what your SA SOP response would have been can be very productive. Look for ways to improve response protocol and rewrite any that need correction. Consider meeting as a group to discuss any events that indicate a trend or escalation that may impact members.

CHAPTER 25

Financial and Legal Considerations

The following information is not a substitute for the advice of legal, financial, and insurance professionals. The reader assumes full responsibility for researching local, state, and federal regulations pertaining to their unique situation.

If you are starting a Survival Alliance, there are some financial and legal things you will need to consider. Like most organizations, there will be money and concerns about liability that you need to establish protocols for. While this is not as interesting as learning advanced first aid or going to the gun range, it is important and will make the group run better. Money is often at the root of many problems that destroy relationships. You don't want the lack of established financial protocol to wreak havoc within the SA, so set these guidelines early on.

Let's begin with the handling of money. Most organized groups such as PTAs or HOAs take in money. They have rules for how that money is handled. These groups generally have a treasurer who keeps the financial books, makes deposits, balances the checking account, and provides regular treasury reports. How much of this standard practice can be applied to your group will depend on factors such as whether you collect funds or have a checking account. Before I go any further, I would like to share some circumstances in which you might choose to deal with money.

Running any group requires effort and money. There are three ways to fund activities and purchases within your SA. The first way to pay for things is **donation**. Members can volunteer to pay for specific communal projects or supplies as they so choose. The second method is the collection of **membership dues**. These funds can be collected yearly, quarterly or monthly. The third way is a combination of the first two. Establish SA policy for who decides how money is spent. If you vote, determine the percentage needed to carry a vote. If using a governing council, you can allow them to decide or have them propose choices on which membership votes. Regardless of who decides, be sure to add the specifics to you Standard Operating Practice guide book. When writing financial SOPs, consider:

- Where will money be stored? Will it be kept by the treasurer or will a bank account be opened? Will any amount be kept for petty cash expenditures? If so, how much? Who dispenses money from petty cash? Will any approval be required prior to dispersal?
- If you use a bank account, how often will deposits be made? Will you require a second signature to issue a group check?
- Who is authorized to make withdrawals?
- How often will be financial officer or treasurer provide a report to the group?
- What happens to money earmarked for a member who moves or is expelled?
- Are there expenses that SA leadership will be reimbursed for?

There are many ways to deal with money. Having said that, money has the potential to tempt, even good people, under the right circumstances. Instituting strict policies, that help members maintain high standards of integrity, is important. This will help protect SA assets and preserve the trust of members.

The most basic concern when it comes to money is security. Where will SA money be kept? The two basic options are in a bank or in private hands. The first option seems counter to the low profile most groups want to maintain, but does have merit. Rather than a checking account, I am suggesting the use of a safe deposit box. A safe deposit box provides a safe, neutral location for larger sums of money without the issues that checking account raise. The person applying for a checking account must supply their social security number and be financially responsible for any applicable tax burden. No one wants to do that. In addition to simplicity and no possible tax liability, a safe deposit box offers privacy. Although it takes two keys to open the box, after turning their key in the lock, bank employees leave the room to allow for privacy.

Safety is another benefit of a **safe deposit box**. Unlike private homes, banks have fewer risks of fire and are stronger buildings. They are more likely to withstand damaging storms. Even if no money is kept in it, a safe deposit box can provide greater security for important documents and keys. If you do store cash, include a ledger for deposits and withdrawals. In this way, if the treasurer is unavailable, records are readily available for the person who fills in for them. A **duplicate ledger** can be signed each time money is added or withdrawn and kept by the SAL for review without having to go to the bank. A duplicate ledger also insures accurate records in case of a falling out with the treasurer.

To hedge the possibility of withdrawal limits or bank closures due to economic crash, purchase the items for which the money was collected as quickly as possible. Office supplies, training and event registration, and big-ticket items should be purchased as soon as the full amount needed is collected. Loading these funds onto a **prepaid credit card** is another way to avoid storing large amounts of cash. This provides the convenience and the buying power of a credit card for online reservations and purchases. Coupled with the use of an SA PO box or PMB (personal mail box) you can pay for and receive deliveries and mail without it going to a members' home. Many seminars and trainings offer discounts for group purchases making this a money saving perk. Purchases I make with our SA card can be sent to the SA PMB. I signed a form that allows the business owner to accept packages, on my behalf, if they don't fit in my mailbox. I chose a PMB that gives me a street address with a suite number. Some businesses will not ship to a PO box and I don't want SA mail coming to my house. To maintain privacy and security, consider naming your SA and having purchases sent to that name as you would a business. Use that name as the club title by adding words like group, club, or association. Depending upon the SA name, you may need an alternate name for use to the obvious nature of the name. Certain words can trigger unwanted attention from state and federal groups. The IRS has been caught flagging groups with conservative titles and delaying or denying their non-profit applications. Choose low profile names to avoid attention.

Alliance name	Mail recipient name
Stonehaven Survival Alliance	Stonehaven Hikers' Club
"Come and Take It" SA	SE Texas Historical Society

Keep in mind that whoever applies for the mailbox must provide their name and show identification and proof of residence. These rules are federally mandated regulations. This allows any criminal activity associated with the use of the address to be traced to a verified owner. Whether this is acceptable will vary from one group to another. Personally, since I am not purchasing anything illegal, I don't mind. Who owns the box should only become an issue if shipments raise suspicion? Using a low-key club or group name will reduce computer generated flagging. Do not impersonate a business. Adding LLC or Inc. could result in legal problems, as they are legal entities requiring state and federal documentation. **To learn what is acceptable in your state, contact an attorney or research the topic online.**

If keeping SA money within the group works best for your SA, insuring it's safety can be approached several ways. The approach you take will depend upon the amount of money you anticipate having on hand at any given time. A petty cash box with twenty to one hundred dollars in mixed currency in it can be kept in a locking file cabinet. In fact, depending upon the location, no lock may be required at all. On the other hand, one thousand dollars being saved for a generator to run the retreat cabin should be kept in a secure location in a locked box or safe. Consider a safe or at least using hidden spaces for storing the cashbox. If your SA collects maintenance dues or regularly collects funds to make online purchases, establish SOPs that determine where money is kept, who has keys or combinations to locks, procedures for making purchases or returning money. Here are some basic policies that should be implemented:

- No purchases will be made with SA funds that was not approved by the governing council or entire group, depending upon the groups' rules.
- All receipts for purchases will be kept and maintained in a file for record keeping and purchased product warranty purposes, where applicable.
- A receipt will be provided for all money received by the financial officer. The reason for the payment will be noted on the receipt for clarification purposes. This should be done using a commercially made receipt book that provides an original and copy for the payor.
- Before funds are added to the cashbox, new funds will be counted by the financial officer **and** an additional member before being added. A deposit slip or entry will be made and signed by both people. These people should not be related or at least not within the immediate family.
- SA policy regarding refunds should be listed in the membership contract and be initialed by applicants in addition to the signature at the end of the document. For the purposes of simplification and fairness, I feel that money paid for maintenance dues, members' share of communal equipment or supplies are **non-refundable**. The only possible exception might be money in escrow for an upcoming SA purchase. If the member is moving out of the appropriate range of the SA or has been expelled from the group, a refund would be fair and simple.

Financial Liability

In keeping with the preparedness mindset, reduction of financial liability should be an integral part of any Survival Alliance. We do this in other aspects of our lives when we purchase auto and home owners' insurance or post signs at home that warns," Beware of dog". We should apply the same effort to SA interactions. We all want to believe that fellow group members would never hold us responsible for an accident at our home, for property stolen from a retreat location or lost to a fire in a storage shed. Additionally, fellow members themselves may honestly believe they would never do so. Despite this sentiment, many friendships and business relationships have ended when an injury or loss of property occurs. It is not uncommon, once the medical bills start rolling in or the replacement items need to be purchased, to find that feelings have changed. It may not even be by choice. Sometimes the medical bills generated by serious injury are beyond the ability of the injured parties' ability to pay. Other times, they may feel they should not have to bear that burden because of perceived negligence on your part. Pain, loss, debt and sometimes greed have a way of convincing many people that it is fair to expect someone else to pay for their unfortunate circumstances. If you are indeed responsible for their injury or loss, they are well within their legal right to expect restitution. If you are not, they may still seek compensation. This restitution could even be court ordered and financially devastating. Being prepared for this possibility is the only way to be sure an accident does not lead to financial ruin.

The first thing to look at is **hazard mitigation**. This term refers to the reduction or elimination of hazards that could lead to injury, death, and damaged, or lost property. This practice is used by municipalities and businesses, and can be applied to private property. I have divided the hazards into three categories; **indoor/outdoor hazards**, **personal property**, and **conduct** related.

Indoor/outdoor hazards and liabilities are those occurring inside and outdoors on your property or during an event you planned and invited others to. When you invite someone to your home or property, it is assumed that you have made reasonable efforts to assure the safety of visitors or guests. Such efforts include, but are not limited to, clearing walkways and sidewalks of snow, ice, debris and tripping hazards, containment of aggressive animals, and cordoning off construction sites, equipment, and supplies that could cause injury. **Regular inspections** of your yard, property, or at your event site can help you spot potential hazards and address them. This is especially important if you have people visit regularly. The more frequently you have guests, the higher the chance of someone hurting themselves.

If you are having a training activity or campout on your property, there will be the additional hazards generated by the activity. If fire will be used, take precautions to reduce accidental spread of flames, burns, and smoke damage or injury. Use flagging tape in neon colors to mark low hanging obstacles, guide wires for tents and canopies, and to cordon off an axe yard. If individuals will be carrying personal blades or using group knives, be sure to cover basic safety, as part of the safety briefing. The Boy Scouts of America offers a simple, yet effective, blade safety training that can be utilized. Search Totem Chip or refer to any Cub or Boy Scout manual for the curriculum which covers safe pocket knife and axe use.

Personal Property and Injury Liability

Emergency preparedness isn't just about tornados and quarantines. It is also protecting yourself from the legal consequences. Bodily injury and property loss of others while on your property or during events you plan can result in financial liability for you. Here are three methods for dealing with these possibilities.

Agreement to hold harmless

An Agreement to Hold Harmless is a simple way to reduce the likelihood that you will be held accountable for another's actions or loss. This is a simple document that you can have all guests or participants sign. It simply states that the participant accepts full responsibility for their safety and agrees to hold the named party blameless. There are several ways that this can be worded. You can find several examples of this wording online. **Consult your attorney** to be sure that the wording you choose is appropriate for the situation you are wanting to cover.

Homeowners' insurance

Whether you own or rent, home and content insurance is the financially responsible way to protect yourself against losses of several types. **Talk to an insurance agent** about possibly increasing your content coverage to be sure you can replace communal equipment, supplies, and structures. **Periodically review coverage** to insure it keeps up with additions of preps or improvements to the property.

Liability Insurance

Liability insurance is coverage for a variety of things for which you may be held responsible. Discuss purchasing an **umbrella policy** with your insurance agent. Umbrella policies are additional coverage purchased to protect the policyholder from lawsuits and major claims that exceed the limits of regular policies such as home owners or auto insurance. In addition to helping cover large monetary settlements, umbrella coverage can cover things not covered in other forms of insurance such as personal injury, slander, libel, defamation of character taking place in your home and can help with the expenses related to your defense. All of this is very complicated and requires a skilled agent. If you have significant assets, consider discussing this type of coverage with your insurance provider. Even if you do not consider yourself wealthy, an umbrella policy may offer you the additional protect you are looking for. We researched it and found it to be very affordable for our business. If you are gracious enough to make your property available to them, they may be willing to help you with your premium. Most lawyers will tell you that this coverage is a smart move. If you are providing a training or bug out location, it seems like a fair trade.

Part of being a responsible adult and being prepared for the unexpected is reducing liability and protecting your finances. Whether this is regular homeowner's or renter's coverage, content insurance or liability insurance, finding coverage that is right for your needs is worth the money.

CHAPTER 26
Encouragement and Summary

Preparedness is an essential part of our life. It can be a source of peace and reassurance to know that you have made plans for the unexpected. These plans can make such events easier to weather. In some cases, these measures can prevent property damage, injury and even death. This is **good stewardship** of the things for which you have responsibility. I believe that the scriptures warn us of things to come so we can be prepared. These warnings are tender mercies from a loving Father. If we heed these warnings, we can be spared needless hardship or better prepared to deal with it. I find peace and courage in the many verses describing what is to come. I pray for discernment to know how what I read applies to my family and what we need to do.

When you first get started, it is easy to feel overwhelmed. Pace yourself and be smart about how you proceed. Even those of us who have been at this a while need to step back and take stock of our efforts. "To everything there is a season and a purpose under the heavens." Ecclesiastes 3:1. For me this means that what I should be focusing on changes from time to time. Some of these changes are related to our age. What I needed to do when we had five young children is different from what I need to do now with only one adult child living with us. What I can physically do as a grandmother is different than what I could do when I was in my twenties. Common sense and inspiration should guide us as we evaluate and re-evaluate our goals.

Differing opinions about preparations within a marriage or family are not uncommon. Sometimes one person has more enthusiasm, interest, or knowledge than others. This can cause frustration between spouses, couples, children, and even SA group members. Here a few tips for more **harmonious prepping**.

- Remember that everyone has unique life experiences that shape how they approach problems. Respecting these differences in opinion is essential to family and group harmony.
- Use current events and reputable sources to educate others. Scare tactics as a primary means of swaying opinion is rarely successful. There are so many logical, rational, and sobering reasons for emergency preparedness, that fear mongering is unnecessary.
- Be patient. Some people have difficulty entertaining events or situations they cannot control or find frightening. If you can navigate these topics calmly and logically, consider yourself blessed. This is a great advantage. Help others in your family and SA through example and patient instruction. Acknowledge fears and concerns while working to encourage growth and confidence.
- Respect limits. Some people have physical, intellectual, or emotional limits that cannot be altered without time and great effort. Some can never overcome their challenges. Look for ways to mitigate the effects of these challenges while providing meaningful ways for them to participate.
- Be thoughtful and generous with praise for any support, progress or growth. My mother always said, "You catch more flies with honey than vinegar."

We hope that this book has given you the basics you need to create a Survival Alliance that works for your needs and those of your loved ones. This information is intended to inspire you to take charge of your safety and well-being and bring you peace of mind. We want to emphasize the need for **moderation and prudence** as you work toward preparedness goals. Extreme measures often create more problems than they solve. Discuss financial decisions with your spouse, significant other and family to be sure their feelings and needs are taken into consideration. In the end, each household should create a custom version of emergency preparedness and their own Survival Alliance. It has been our pleasure to introduce this concept to you and hope that it will save you money and stress, as you create safer ways to weather the ups and downs of life.

We would love to hear from you. If you have questions or suggestions, please contact us at survivalalliances@gmail.com. We invite you to visit our website at **SurvivalAlliances.com** to check out the newest tips, videos, and products to help you with your SA goals. We will be unveiling Booster Packs for your SA Binder and a new book on raising prepared children soon. **SURVIVAL ALLIANCES** is a family run business dedicated to promoting emergency preparedness.

The following forms have been designed to help you organize and administer your own SA, if you so choose. You can use them as is, or as aids in developing your own. There is no time like the present, so get to it! **A year from now you will wish you had started prepping today.**

Survival Alliance Administrative Forms

- SA Scouting Information Sheet
- SA Skills Survey
- SA Admission Requirement Work Sheet
- New Member Orientation/Contract
- SA Privacy Agreement
- SA Skill Group Roster
- SA Alert System Samples
- Family Communication Plan Example
- SA Communication Plan Example

SA Scouting Information Sheet

Name _____   Address _____

_____

_____

Cell Phone _____   Home Phone _____

Age _____ DOB _____   Spouse _____ Age _____

Kids _____

Employer _____   Occupation _____

Hobbies _____   Memberships _____

Fitness level / Limitations _____

Known medical history _____

Political Affiliation _____   Religion _____

Weapons Experience. None _____ Novice _____ Proficient _____ Trained _____

      Type _____

Hunting experience_____

Military training _____

Medical training _____

Notes _____

_____

_____

_____

Referred by _____

Team Leader _____   Disposition _____

Alliance Skill Survey

I = Interest   E = Experience   T = Training

Name _____ Date _____ SGL _____

Security / Defense
Law Enforcement
Department _____ Rank _____ Duration _____ Position _____

Military
Service _____ Rank _____ Duration _____ Discharge _____

MOS _____

Private
Security _____ Investigator _____ Alarm / Surveillance _____ Computer Security Skills _____

Skills
Handgun ____ Rifle ____ Shotgun ____ Full/Semi ____ Explosives ____ Intelligence ____
Self Defense ____ Martial Artist ____ Style / Rank ____ Concealed Carry ____ Lock Pick ____
Scouting ____ Tracking ____ Disguise ____

Special Training _____

Medical
First Aid _____
Basic ___ Advanced ___ Medic ___ EMT ___ Paramedic ___ CNA ____ LPN ___ RN ___ MD ___ Chiropractor ___ PT ___ OT ___

Special Needs Care:
Experienced care giver for: Infants ___ Children ___ Physically Disabled ___
Cognitively Disabled ___ Elderly ___
Pressure wounds ___ Skin Tears ___ Patient Transfers ___ Peri Care ___ Gait Assistance ___ Bed Bath ___ Occupied
Bed Change ___ Feeding ___ Diabetic Care ___ Seizure Response ___ Severe Allergies/Anaphylaxis ___ Celiac Disease ___
Gluten Allergy ___ other_____

Skills: _____

_____

Alternative Medicine
Essential Oils _____ Herbs _____ Making Herbal Medicine _____ Homeopathic _____
Massage Therapy _____ Acupuncture / Pressure _____ Reiki _____ Muscle Testing _____

Other _____

Mechanical/Technical/Trades

Engine Repair: Small _____ Auto _____ Diesel _____ Tractor _____ Industrial _____

Welding _____ Metal Working _____ Framing _____ Construction _____

Electrical: Residential _____ Commercial _____ Industrial _____ Automotive _____

Computer _____ Engineering _____ Architect _____ Ham Radio _____ Phone _____

Food Prep/Preservation

Chef ____ Large Family Cook ____ Camp Cook ____ Rocket Stove ____ Dakota Fire Pit ____

Grill Master ____ Smoking ____ Canning ____

Beverage Making: Soda ____ Kombucha ____ Beer____ Wine ____ Liquor____ Fermentation ____

Wild Game Prep ____ Fish/Seafood ____ Organizing Camp Kitchen ____

Outdoor Skills

Boy or Venture Scouts ____ Yrs. _____ Fire Starting ____ Tent Pitching ____ Basic Knots ____

Grilling ____ Dutch Oven Cooking ____ Rocket Stove ____ Solar Oven ____ Orienteering ____

Hiking ____ Rock Climbing/Repelling ____ Boating ____ Canoe/Kayaking ____ Bush Craft ____

Horseback Riding ____ Finding Water ____ Purifying Water ____

Other _____

Character References

Please provide the references of one non applicant family member, two friends, and at least one from your association within the community such as church, a scouting organization, civic group, hobby, or sports team. Letters should indicate how the writer knows you and for how long, as well as his or her opinion of your character and performance within the context of your association with them.

Comments

_____

_____

_____

_____

_____

Admission Requirement Work Sheet

Candidate Name: _____

Background check completed and attached: _____

Character references completed and attached: _____

Requirement	Quantity	Goal Deadline
Food		
Water		
Gear		
Skills		
Training		

NEW MEMBER ORIENTATION

Welcome to the _____Survival Alliance.

Your acceptance into this group indicates that you have fulfilled the membership and character requirements of the Alliance. We commend you for your hard work and integrity. We look forward to working with you to help yourself, your family, and the group to become better prepared to meet whatever the future holds.

The following are basic policies that govern the Survival Alliance.

1. Our most important rule is to **NEVER** discuss the SA with non members. For everyone's safety, do not engage in conversations about the SA and/or its activities. No mention of the SA should be made through any medium, i.e. phone, text, email, social media, around others, or in the presence of smart phones.

2. When referring to the SA in unsecured circumstances, refer to the group as _____ and the meeting as _____.

3. For security purposes, do not refer to other members by their name around non members. It would be possible for others to "connect the dots" through social media, friends online, or in groups such as church. This protects everyone.

4. **NEVER** bring non members to an Alliance meeting.

5. If you have a 'candidate for membership' suggestion, fill out a Survival Alliance Scouting Sheet and submit it to an SGL. The membership committee will then discuss the candidate with you. If approved for further vetting, the Committee will advise you on how and when to introduce the candidate to The SA.

6. Please maintain your food and water supplies, gear, and skills. Periodic inspections are conducted to ensure that all members are able to fulfill their roles within the SA.

7. If any changes occur in your demographics i.e. phone numbers, address, or employment please inform the communications officer. Communication among members is vitally important.

8. If you are a provisional member, inform your SA leader if you have a situation that restricts you from completing your goals. Revision of your completion dates may be possible.

9. Do not post pictures of any SA members online unless those pictures are of public events apart from SA events. Such examples are baseball games, scouting, or weddings.

10. Please submit certificates of completion for all training that generates one or report completion of those that don't to the training officer. You Skill Acquisition file will then be updated.

11. In communal settings such as training, camping, sheltering in place, or bugging out, please show respect for the privacy of others as much as is possible.

12. Verbal abuse, intimidation, physical violence, sexual harassment, or infidelity has no place among SA members. They erode the trust and confidence needed for members to function efficiently. If a situation arises between members that cannot be resolved peacefully, report it to the Morale officer or an SA leader.

13. Membership in the SA requires adherence to the policies and procedures for all members, regardless of position. All members are required to abide by the decisions of the leadership board. Failure to do so may lead to consequences such as retraining, fines, additional tasks, reassignment, or expulsion from the SA.

Signature: _____

Print: _____

Date: _____

(Give copy to member and file original. One form per person)

Privacy Agreement

I, _____, understand the need for discretion and security regarding The Survival Alliance. I will abide by the OPSEC guidelines at all times and will report any violations I observe within the group to my group leader. I understand that I am subject to the consequences associated with breeches of Survival Alliance security, including expulsion from the group. I pledge my allegiance to The Alliance and its mission and its members.

Furthermore, I also understand that if I choose to resign from the Alliance that I will continue to abide by all OPSEC policies.

Signature: _____

Print: _____

Date: _____

Witness: _____

SA Alert System Samples

Number System

Level 1 – Normal – maintain regular routine and preparedness

Level 2 – Slightly elevated vigilance – Follow trusted news sources

Level 3 – Significant possible threat – Keep cash on hand, top off perishables and basic preps and stay tuned to trusted news sources.

Level 4 – Imminent threat – Prepare to shelter in place or bug-out (depending on whichever is most appropriate). Consider removing money from bank, topping off gas supplies, buying any supplies/food needed for prolonged event, purchase ammo if needed. Begin home security measures.

Level 5 – Bug-out or shelter in place. All defensive measures in place

Color System

Green – All good – Normal routine

Yellow – Possible threat identified – follow issue closely

Orange – Threat impact verified – Top off food, medical, fuel and technical supply.
Prepare to shelter in place/ bug-out. Activate appropriate defensive measures and stay tuned to trusted news sources.

Red – Prepare for imminent threat impact (weather, economic, criminal, military) Implement safety measures for home, property, and family.

Family Communication Plan

In the event of an emergency, the following procedure will be used for members of this household to check in and receive instructions.

Emergency Response

- If an emergency occurs during the business day while everyone is in different locations, the family members affected will text _____ their location and condition. Example- Cameron-Science class, A building, on lock down, I'm fine.

- _____ or a parent will text instructions for each member as to pick up or sheltering in place.

- If the event is a large scale emergency, and all members will call or text _____ listed as ICE in your phone. Leave your location, condition, and any plans to move.

- Special instructions for young children

_____

_____

_____

Fire Response

- Fire extinguishers are located in the kitchen by _____

  and/or in the _____ by the _____.

- Do not use water on grease. Smother fire with pot lid and remove from heat. Use properly rated extinguisher for electrical fires.

- If we have to evacuate the house because of fire, everyone will meet at the _____.

- When you leave the house, go straight to the designated meeting place and **DO NOT LEAVE.** If anyone is missing, it will be assumed that they are still in the house. **CALL 911.**

Hurricane / Tornado Plan

- When severe weather is forecasted the weather radio will be on at any time the television is not.

- If an adult is not home, the weather radio will be turned on during severe weather regardless of whether the television is on.

- If travel to/or from school may be dangerous, children will stay home with _____.

- If a tornado warning is issued, anyone in the house will go to the _____ and take _____.

- Family members will wear long pants and closed toed shoes during severe storm capable of producing tornadoes'

- If personal go bags are not stored in a storm shelter, each family member should take their bag to the designated safe area once tornado danger is announced in the area.

- If in a public place, such as the grocery store, during a tornado warning, go to the

_____.

Notes

_____

_____

_____

_____

_____

SA Communication Plan Example

Remember the regional weather events and issues particular to your area when creating your Communication Plan. Keep in mind local sites that could be targets for terrorism or would be dangerous if there were a fire or damage to the building. Plan multiple evacuation routes from your city and metro area to your bug out location; if you should have one. Research city evacuation plans, snow routes, and low water crossings. Pay special attention to traffic flow around your area. Some routes could cause a traffic bottle neck and prevent evacuation.

- SA members will maintain appropriate storm response gear in order to be able to care for their family and respond to other members, if needed.

- For most weather related events, members will shelter in place and check in with their SGL once a day to give their status report. If the weather is severe and prolonged, check in morning and evening.

- If loss of power for a prolonged period of time is expected, members should consider consolidating to preserve resources and have the support of other members.

- All members who have storm shelters should report its' location to the SAL and their SGL as well as the member living closest to them. In the event that storm debris litters the property, first responders will be better able to locate and clear the hatch.

- Members should share their family or household communication plan with their SGL. The printed plan will be filed in the member file to be accessed in an emergency.

Survival Alliance Checklists

- Recommended Clothing by Category
- Clothing & Fabric Gear Repair Kit
- Mechanical and Technical Repair
- Post- Disaster Supply Kit
- Boredom Buster Kit

Recommended Clothing by Category

Protective

_____Ladies aprons and smocks for light duty use

_____Men's aprons for metal working

_____Waterproof apron to keep clothing dry

_____Wash gloves, both light and heavy duty

_____Canvas gloves for light duty protection

_____Leather gloves for friction producing tasks

_____Mechanic gloves for high dexterity jobs

_____Sun bonnets to shade face and back of neck

_____Wide brimmed hats – straw/canvas with chin cinch

_____Bandanas for shade, sweat band, mask, filter

_____Insoles for various types of shoes

Name	Item	Maker	Model	Source	Cost

Notes

Cold Weather Wear

_____Thermal underwear   _____Balaclavas

_____Sweaters   _____Knit caps

_____Light jackets   _____Fudd hats

_____Heavy jackets   _____Scarves

_____Snow pants / bibs   _____Hand warmers

_____Snow boots   _____Body warmers

_____Snow gloves   _____Wool socks

Name	Shirt Size	Pant Size	Shoe Size	# Needed	# On Hand

Under Garments

_____Underwear

_____Under shirts

_____Bras (consider sports bras)

_____Sport camisoles

_____Crew socks

_____Compression socks

_____Sock liners for hiking

Daily Wear Clothing

_____Light color, long sleeved shirts for sun protection

_____Jeans / canvas pants – some with cargo pockets

_____Shorts / Capris - cargo style are sturdy and helpful

_____T shirts – long and short sleeves

Name	Underwear Size	Bra Size	Sock Size	# Needed	# On Hand

Notes

_____

_____

_____

_____

Clothing and Fabric Gear Repair

_____Thread in regular and heavy-duty weight

_____Sewing needles in a variety of sizes

_____Upholstery needs for heavy fabric and leather

_____Crewel and needle point needles for woven items

_____Thimbles to protect your finger/ thumb

_____Buttons in various sizes and colors

_____Zippers of different length and colors

_____Elastic in a variety of widths and tensions

_____Denim patch fabric both iron-on and sew on

_____Darning egg or ball or substitute a wooden craft ball

_____Extra Fabric and sewing patterns for basic garments

_____Crochet and knitting needles/yarn

_____Sewing machine for use with generator or a pedal

Item	Part	Model	&	Number	# Needed	# On Hand

Notes

Repair for Gear (tents, backpacks, canopies etc.)

_____Water repellant spray

_____Seam waterproofing for tents and rain gear

_____Grommet replacement kit

_____Super glues for different purposes

_____Regular and self -stick Velcro

_____Regular and self -stick Velcro

_____Extra para cord and tent stakes

_____Extra mallet for pounding stakes

_____Safety pins in various sizes – good quality

_____Duct tape in silver, black and camo pattern

_____JB Weld for heat tolerant repairs to metal clasps

_____Nylon rope / para cord for tents

_____Extra tent bag or duffle bag for tent/canopy

_____Heavy duty needle and thread for canvas repair

Item	Part	Model	&	Number	# Needed	# On Hand

Notes

Mechanical & Electrical Repair

_____Eyeglass repair kit – inexpensive, so buy several

_____Eyeglass cords to prevent dropping

_____2 or 3 sets of small screwdriver for electronics/ battery hatches

_____Needle nose pliers

_____Wire cutters

_____Wire strippers

_____Assorted gauges of electrical wire

_____Soldering iron and related supplies

_____Voltage meter

_____Electrical tape- multiple colors

_____Owner manuals for all equipment in folder by type

_____Downloaded scheduled maintenance guide

_____Haynes, Chilton, or other repair guide for your specific vehicles

_____Grease, oils, and lubricants for machinery and engines

_____Spare belt, gaskets, filters and rings

_____Assortment of bolts, washers and nuts for important gear

_____Assortment of generic household hardware

_____Full tool set in metric sizes

_____Full tool set in standard sizes

_____Measurement Conversion Chart

_____Extra screw drivers, crescent wrenches, sockets and socket wrenches

_____Parts for tune up on main vehicle

_____Belts and hoses for main vehicle

_____JB Weld (I can't say enough good things about it)

_____Measuring tape

_____Air tanks – for tires

_____Compressor

_____Tire gauge

_____Flat repair kit

_____Bike inner tubes and repair kit

_____Tool boxes

_____WD 40 or similar spray lubricant

_____"Choke spray"

_____Motor oil, filter, filter wrench, air filters

_____Rags for wiping oily parts and hands on

_____Mechanics hand cleaner will reduce water needed to wash.

Item	Part	Model	&	Number	# Needed	# On Hand

Notes

Post-Disaster Response Kit

Unless you have had experience with a variety of emergency or disaster situations, it's hard to know what little things can make life a bit more bearable. Here are some suggestions gathered from first responders, families with critically ill members, and some experienced preppers.

Rise and Shine!

- Toothbrush in a case and trial size toothpaste
- Instant coffee packets or small jar of freeze dried
- Hair ties or barrettes to put hair up
- Lip balm and tube of moisturizer
- Breakfast or granola bars trail mix
- Add prescription and OTC meds to kit when needed

- _____

- _____

Helping Hands

- Work gloves for recovery and clean- up work
- Pocket size hand sanitizer and refill bottle
- Sponge ear plugs to dampen equipment noise
- Ziploc bag of medical gloves
- Small spiral notebook for notes in the field
- Sunglasses and cap or visor for outdoor work
- First aid kit with tweezers and nail clippers
- Bandana for tons of purposes
- Waterproof sunblock
- Bug repellant
- Pocket knife
- Water bottle
- Safety vest

- _____

- _____

Hurry up and wait

Many events that we prepare for can result in a lot of time on our hands. Preparing for this in advance will make these more common episodes of waiting much less stressful, especially for kids.

- Spiral note book and pen
- paperback novel
- travel scriptures
- Travel size pillow or neck rest
- Coloring book and colored pencils
- Sudoku, crossword, or word search
- Battery brick or charger pack and cord
- Earphones for phone, computer, or tablet
- Hand held game or game system & charger
- Emergency contact addresses and phone numbers
- Trail mix, beef jerky or fruit snacks
- Battery Brick for charging cell phone/lap top

- _____

- _____

Time to hit the hay

- Sponge earplugs– reduces generator noise/snoring
- Eye mask in case you need to sleep during the day
- Body powder – medicated type soothes and cools
- Polar fleece or micro fiber T.V. blanket
- Travel pillow or neck rest
- Baby wipes for duck baths
- Hand and body warmers in winter
- Topical medication for sore muscles
- Ibuprophen or other anti-inflammatory
- Allergy medication

- _____

- _____

Boredom Buster Box Check List

Babies and toddlers

- Balls- solid, rubber, tennis balls,
- Simple stuffed animals
- Rattle or jingle toy and teething toys
- Simple toys with wheels that can be pulled or pushed

Young children- up to age 8

- Dolls with clothing and accessories for role playing such as bottle or carrier
- Trucks and cars – construction variety is especially good for outdoor play
- Building blocks or plastic linking blocks and idea pictures or book
- Outdoor toys such as jump rope, hoola hoop, jacks, marbles with game ideas and rules
- Hopscotch, 4 square, bike riding – sidewalk chalk is cheap and has many outdoor uses
- Dress up – collect simple costume basics in a plastic bin with a lid. Wands, crowns and tiaras, capes, masks that cover eye area, cowboy hat, fairy wings, police or sheriff badges, toy guns or bow and arrow.
- Card games such as memory and matching games, Old Maid, or simple board games.
- Simple jigsaw puzzles, coloring books and crayons or colored pencils, books, copier paper

Tweens, Teens and Adults

- Chapter books and novels
- Journals and art supplies like markers and stickers
- Whittling – appropriate pocket knife, sharpening stone, patterns and basic instructions
- Origami – Fun and challenging, gender neutral activity. Be sure to store instructions, rulers, & paper.
- Store yarn or twine for string games lie cats' cradle or Jacobs' ladder along with instructions.
- Yarn can also be used for knitting and crochet. Again, store instructions and patterns.
- Musical instruments such as recorders, ocarinas, harmonicas and mouth harps are inexpensive and although old fashioned, can bring hours of enjoyment. Once mastered they can entertain others.
- Puzzles – large, challenging ones are great for communal spaces and encourage people to sit and visit while they work. This can be a great stress reliever and provide chances for individuals to bond.

Boredom Buster Box Supplies

- Ball of smooth twine or yarn (string games and marbles)
- Skeins of yarn (needle work)
- Playing cards
- Children's' card games (Old Maid, Memory)
- Ream of copy paper (drawing, origami, writing)
- Crayons, colored pencils and pencils (crayons melt)
- Scissors

- Craft glue
- Rulers and retractable measuring tapes
- Assorted books for various ages, including scriptures
- Jump ropes – single, double Dutch and Chinese with list of rhymes or songs that accompany jumping
- Crossword and word search books (dollar stores have lots to choose from)
- Harmonica, recorder, ocarina, mouth harp and simple arrangements of familiar songs
- Copies of hymns – make booklets of your favorites for everyone in your family
- Collection of sing-a-long songs with multiple copies
- Marbles and rules for several games
- Sidewalk chalk for sidewalk games
- Jacks and instructions for playing
- Instructions for making paper boats, paper hats, grass blade whistle etc.

Name	Specific Item	Goal Date	Complete

Notes

_____

_____

_____